Kamal Javanmard
Amir Nasr Khazraei
Mohsen Mohammadi

Role of the Prosecutor in Pursuing Economic Crimes

Kamal Javanmard
Amir Nasr Khazraei
Mohsen Mohammadi

Role of the Prosecutor in Pursuing Economic Crimes

in the Administrative System of the Country

Noor Publishing

Imprint

Any brand names and product names mentioned in this book are subject to trademark, brand or patent protection and are trademarks or registered trademarks of their respective holders. The use of brand names, product names, common names, trade names, product descriptions etc. even without a particular marking in this work is in no way to be construed to mean that such names may be regarded as unrestricted in respect of trademark and brand protection legislation and could thus be used by anyone.

Cover image: www.ingimage.com

Publisher:
Noor Publishing
is a trademark of
Dodo Books Indian Ocean Ltd. and OmniScriptum S.R.L publishing group

120 High Road, East Finchley, London, N2 9ED, United Kingdom
Str. Armeneasca 28/1, office 1, Chisinau MD-2012, Republic of Moldova, Europe
Printed at: see last page
ISBN: 978-620-5-63432-5

Role of the Prosecutor in Pursuing Economic Crimes in the Administrative System of the Country

By

Dr. Kamal Javanmard

Member of The Academic Staff of The Islamic Azad University, Shahr Quds Branch, The Deputy of The Islamic Azad University, Safadasht Branch, Iran

Dr. Amir Nasr Khazraei

Lecturer at Javid Jiroft University, Iran

Mohsen Mohammadi

PhD Student in Public Law at Islamic Azad University, Kish Branch, Lecturer and Legal Expert at Islamic Azad University, Safadasht Branch, Iran

Ahmad Amir Sharifi

PhD Student in Public Law, Islamic Azad University, Kish branch, a Basic Lawyer of a Court, Iran

Ruholah Bor Bor

Lawyer and Civil Activist, Iran

Dr. Kamal Javanmard

Member of The Academic Staff of The Islamic Azad University, Shahr Quds Branch, The Deputy of The Islamic Azad University, Safadasht Branch, Iran

Dr. Amir Nasr Khazraei

Lecturer at Javid Jiroft University, Iran

Mohsen Mohammadi

PhD Student in Public Law at Islamic Azad University, Kish Branch, Lecturer and Legal Expert at Islamic Azad University, Safadasht Branch, Iran

Ahmed Amir Sharifi

PhD Student in Public Law, Islamic Azad University, Kish branch, a Basic Lawyer of a Court, Iran

Ruholah Bor Bor

Lawyer and Civil Activist, Iran

Content

Abstract

Since the occurrence of economic crimes mostly affects all members of the society and is of a special complexity and is carried out by certain people, for this reason, the prosecution and trial of economic defendants is not dependent on the filing of a complaint by a private plaintiff, and the prosecutor's office is obliged to prosecute and declare a crime against the defendants. On the one hand, economic crimes lead to the concentration of capital and increase the gap between the rich and the poor, and on the other hand, this accumulation of capital causes its instrumental use to facilitate and increase the commission of other crimes, and as a result, hindering economic progress and jeopardizing the economic security of society. The occurrence of economic crimes is a problem for all members of the society and the victims of these crimes are generally the people, which will not be possible unless the independence of the prosecutor is preserved in the sense of the freedom of the prosecutor from any interference and influence from those in power. This concept requires that the prosecutor and the prosecutor's institution be supported against external pressures and that no power and authority interfere in it, and only the criteria of justice and justice prevail in it. Judgment criteria should be formed based on justice-oriented perceptions of laws and regulations, not recommendations and exercise of powers and influence. Therefore, in order for the prosecutor to be able to work in line with his goals in the way of preventing and fighting economic crimes, the judiciary and even other forces must have a series of tools and requirements such as the methods of selecting and appointing prosecutor judges, independence from sources of power and also, the employees and officers of the prosecutor's office should be provided to help the prosecutor to pursue economic crimes.

Key words: *Prosecutor, Economic Crimes, Independence of the Prosecutor's Office, Influence, Power Holders.*

Chapter I

Introduction

Introduction

In this book, the role of the prosecutor in investigations related to administrative and financial corruption is reviewed. According to the statistics presented by the organizations that investigate the administrative corruption of the countries of the world, it can be seen that the phenomenon of administrative and financial corruption is considered as an important danger for societies and humanity. The indicators related to Iran show that the situation of our country in the field of corruption control is unfavorable. Therefore, it is necessary to try to recognize this phenomenon and provide appropriate solutions. Researches related to administrative and financial corruption can be classified around four main topics: definitions, consequences, solutions and measurement of corruption.

Financial and administrative corruption is a historical, large, influential phenomenon and the focus of thinking and policy making. Today, administrative and financial corruption has become a global problem. Governments are aware that corruption causes many damages and knows no boundaries, just as its results and consequences are different according to the type of political and economic organization and the level of development.

In today's world, especially in developing countries, this phenomenon has been raised as one of the most important factors in the way of society's progress, and it causes irreparable damage to the speed of movement of society's development wheel. Unfortunately, the available studies show that the phenomenon of corruption is the most among poor and developing countries in these countries. Iran is the first developing country and because of the characteristics that are listed as countries prone to corruption and among the suitable environments for corruption to occur. Also, to the extent that economic activities are developed in the country and if the necessary measures are not taken to fight, the grounds of corruption will be strengthened.

The importance and necessity of conducting research

Although theoretical discussions about corruption took a more serious form in the 1950s, the first theoretical works and empirical studies on corruption were presented from the 1970s, and since then it has been one of the main discussions in the field of government, governance and development. Corruption in the administrative systems of most countries has caused serious damage to development and progress, and in developing countries, the importance of its containment and control has become clear to politicians and their people. Administrative corruption weakens the belief of nations in their ability and causes disappointment and disillusionment in the foreseeable future.

Corruption leads to an increase in transaction prices and disrupts sustainable development and predictability. As a result, the fight against administrative corruption is a necessity to prevent future damage. The Supreme Leader of the Revolution (2006) states in relation to the importance of dealing with corruption: The worst corruption in society is the spread of poverty and the widening of the gap between the rich and the poor. The worst corruption in the society is when people get financial and economic corruption and feed from the people's wealth for their personal benefits and to fill their pockets. The biggest corruption is that there is discrimination in the implementation and application of the law in the society and not paying attention to the competences and abilities of individuals. Corruption is a social phenomenon and not only related to a specific person, because its effects affect the society.

In this regard, the Supreme Leader (2006) states: financial and economic corruption in the formations of the responsible officials and among them spreads to the country's economic body, so it must be prevented. Attention to this work is due to the fact that economic corruption is a polluted flow that if not prevented and fought, it will pollute the entire space.

It is not a single and isolated crime, dealing with economic corruption is vitally important for the system. The principle of social justice, the implementation of justice, considering the rights of the vast masses of people and filling the class gap is one of the main principles of the Islamic system. In the system of the Islamic Republic of Iran, the fight against administrative corruption and economic corruption and abuse of the facilities that the power gives to individuals, whether it is financial abuse or political abuse, are the principles of the revolution and must be observed. Fighting corruption is a main and fundamental issue. Economic corruption in government institutions causes the profits of all the efforts made in the direction of progress and production of public wealth for the welfare of the people to flow into the pockets of a few people who take advantage and abuse what, so the fight against corruption is serious.

The spread of financial corruption is rightly considered as one of the most important obstacles to economic progress, and the high level of financial corruption can lead to the inefficiency of government policies. Researches show that corruption causes a decrease in investment and thus pushes economic activities from being productive to rents and underground activities.

Widespread corruption is one of the signs of weak governance, although weak governance can directly weaken the process of economic growth and development. On the other hand, due to the importance of the problems and risks of administrative and financial corruption for the stability and security of society and democratic institutions and values, moral values and justice, sustainable development and the rule of law, and also due to the link between corruption and other human misbehavior and social and organized crimes, fight against corruption is necessary. As the most important factor, the judiciary and the prosecutor are responsible for monitoring and following up on these issues, and in this book, we examine and analyze these duties.

Literature review and related record

In research, the relationship between administrative corruption and good governance has been investigated. The results of the aforementioned research show that corruption is affected by the type of government's relationship with other sectors and its role, position and special work in the society, and hence it introduces the model of good governance as a new model in order to reduce corruption and increase administrative health.

Qalipour (2004) in the study of the relationship between corruption control and good governance reaches the conclusion that the more the level of governance improves, the more corruption is controlled and administrative health increases. In other words, corruption control has a direct relationship with good governance. Some of the indicators that affect administrative corruption are:

- ❖ Political rights and civil liberties: There is a negative correlation between political rights and civil liberties and corruption.

- ❖ The right to express opinions and participate: Policy making and implementation of large government projects should be done by taking into account the opinions of stakeholders and the participation of all stakeholders. Because the survey of citizens, which includes their feedback, has helped to improve the performance of the public sector and reduce corruption in many countries of the world.

- ❖ Transparency and public supervision: The transparency of the timely and reliable flow of economic, social and political information about the use of loans by private investors and the credit values of borrowers, government services, financial and monetary policies and the activities of international institutions. provides international Studies show that the lack of transparency causes the formation of financial, administrative and policy crises.

- ❖ Competition and free entry and exit: One of the sources of corruption, especially at senior management levels, is the concentration of power in the hands of people who use their political influence in the government for personal gain. To solve this problem, de-monopoly, de-regulation, facilitating competition and entry and exit through liquidation of assets and efficient procedures are suitable solutions.

Abdurrahman Afzali (2013) in the article "Administrative corruption and its effect on development: causes, consequences and solutions" explained the role of administrative corruption in societies and its effect on development, and by entering its conceptual literature, defined corruption in particular administrative corruption, which is the main obstacle to development and the source of other corruptions, and then points to the levels, types and concept of corruption in international documents. Then, in a short discussion, he states the causes and effective factors in administrative corruption, and while comparing the state of administrative corruption in the world and in Iran, he states the consequences and strategies to combat this destructive phenomenon.

In the research conducted by Mohsen Farhadinejad under the title "Investigation of administrative corruption and its control methods". The findings of the research show that the economic situation, culture, individual and organizational characteristics, quality and quantity of laws and regulations are the most important factors in administrative violations. Also, the results of this survey showed that several factors, including increasing the rights of the public sector, establishing effective regulations and laws, public awareness of regulations and laws, efficient financial systems, reforming the administrative structure, non-politicization of the administrative system and privatization can control and prevent administrative violations to be effective.

Mohin Dekht Kazemi in his research entitled "administrative and economic corruption in Iran, solutions" has tried to explain the background of this political, economic and social problem in Iran, how to deal with it at different times and the causes of this problem and offers solutions to reduce or remove it.

Mohammad Khezri has argued in the article "pathology of the methods of fighting against administrative corruption in Iran" that the main reason for the failure of the government's actions and efforts or their low effectiveness lies in the damages that are ignored or underestimated in the fight against the phenomenon of administrative corruption become the main harms that have been analyzed in this article are: the moralistic approach to administrative corruption, the generalization error of

Weber's bureaucracy, secrecy and avoidance of transparency in dealing with administrative corruption, disregarding the citizens' demand aspect of administrative corruption, bureaucratic authority , the distortion of client's rights and its high fragility in the country's bureaucracy, compassionate struggle in the environment of rent, centralized ownership of the media and press and the application of government restrictions on the amount and quality of their reporting, incomplete use of market-oriented methods, pressure from individuals and special groups to prevent the serious pursuit of the fight against administrative corruption and lack of trust in independent anti-corruption institutions and organizations.

Mohammad Ali Mushfaq in the article "social pathology of administrative and economic corruption in Iran" first discusses the issue of corruption from different perspectives and then points out the administrative and legal factors effective in causing corruption and finally the factors affecting It analyzes administrative corruption.

Sayyid Omid Ghazi Asgar (۲۰۱۰) investigated the duties and powers of the prosecutor in civil affairs, the summary of which is as follows. The subject of this research is the duties and powers of the prosecutor in civil affairs. This treatise is organized in three parts: The first part of this treatise is dedicated to introducing the structure of the fictional institution and the historical history of this institution in Iranian and French law. The topic of the second part of this treatise is devoted to the scope of the prosecutor's involvement in civil affairs and the characteristics of the prosecutor's institution, and in the third part, the researcher deals with the examples of the prosecutor's involvement in civil affairs and the main tasks and duties of the prosecutor in matters belonging to prisoners, absent persons, property and discusses the process of civil proceedings.

Chapter II

Generalities

In order to examine the role of the prosecutor in the pursuit of economic crimes in the administrative system of the country, it is necessary to first introduce the prosecutor and the judicial system in the first topic, introducing the attorney general, emphasizing the duties of the general system in protecting public rights in the event of economic crimes in the topic. Second, considering the importance of interaction and cooperation of other institutions with the prosecutor in the pursuit of economic crimes in the administrative system, the third topic should examine the role of the prosecutor general's office in creating reflection with other institutions in pursuing and fighting economic crimes and the enforcement of public rights.

Topic 1: Introducing the prosecutor and the judicial system

In order to introduce the prosecutor and the prosecution system, it is necessary to first address the background and coordinates of the prosecution system and then the general duties of the story when economic crimes occur.

The first speech: background and coordinates of the judicial system

The prosecutor or the public prosecutor is a judicial authority who performs duties to protect public rights and supervise the implementation of laws according to legal regulations. In cases where the crime does not have a private plaintiff and has caused damage to society in some way, the prosecutor will file a lawsuit on behalf of the people against the perpetrators.

According to article 49 of the Law on principles of judiciary organizations, the holder of the office of prosecutor is a judge who is responsible for protecting public rights and supervising the implementation of laws, and according to article 50 of this law, he has the authority of a public attorney in criminal trials. For this reason, he is sometimes called a public lawyer. generally, when the prosecutor is mentioned, an organization called the prosecutor's office comes to mind, and the prosecutor carries out his duties under that organization.

An institution that has its roots in the history of France and its history goes back to the 14th century AD. When people under the title of public prosecutor or public lawyer were responsible for representing the king to protect the interests of the government and the king before the court. These people also appear in courts to defend the interests of the government, especially tax interests. The word "parque", which is still used in French-speaking countries in the sense of the prosecutor's office, in a way reflects this era, when the representatives of kings, like any other ordinary plaintiff, were forced to state their claim standing on the wooden floor of the courts, and a special chair or tribune for reading. They didn't have a letter, but now prosecutors are standing as judges in many countries.

In France, in 1808, an organization was created to control the actions of the police, which in a way had the initial form of the prosecutor's office. If we want to observe the dignity and relevance of the establishment of the prosecution institution, I must admit that the prosecution is an institution in the set of legal systems of the world, a judiciary that without having the right of trial performs its duties in order to prepare the public indictment and facilitate the proceedings of the court, of course Rarely, in some judicial systems, the prosecutor's office is not in the presence of the court and complements it, but because England may be related to the police institution, due to the dependence and connection of the police's investigative activities with the prosecution of crimes, this professional relationship is carried out by a quasi-judicial official and the police, that is, the prosecutor, is done.

In accordance with the judicial system governing the countries, the judicial system is managed under the supervision of the attorney general or even the minister with the chief justice.

If in France, court judges enter the court system at the suggestion of the Minister of Justice and the issuance of a sentence by the president and without the intervention of the supreme council of judges, while the judgments of court judges are issued by the supreme council of judges. What is current in the mixed and mixed legal systems of the world, which have accepted prosecutors in the presence of the court, is that since crime is a social phenomenon and has social consequences. Therefore, the right to prosecute a crime belongs to the society, and the society implements this right through its representatives from time to time.

The prosecutor's office is the representative of society and prosecutes criminals in the name of society. The duty of the prosecutor's office is to defend the society, defend the law and defend the right. In the systems where the prosecutor's office is accepted, referring to the court is either limited to certain times and conditions or is generally prohibited and ruled out. In the recent method, criminal lawsuits must first be raised in the prosecutor's office, and after collecting the evidence, for and against the accused, and conducting preliminary investigations, the prosecutor's office officials send a request to the court with the issuance of a penalty.

 In our country, after the constitutional revolution and the establishment of customary courts, which were also sealed with the seal of approval of the first-rate constitutional scholars, the prosecutor's office under the title of the public prosecutor's office was considered to be one of the most important criminal institutions in the country. If it is objected, this institution is foreseen in the law on the principles of judiciary organizations and the lawyer of the congregation is included as a judicial authority in its decision.

According to this law and other complementary laws, duties such as filing lawsuits and prosecuting crimes and defendants in terms of public rights, as well as the rights of the government, indigent persons and missing persons, have been assigned to the public prosecutor. This institution continued to exist until ۱۹۹۵, but with the drafting of the law on the formation of public courts and the revolution, the prosecutor's office was removed from the general criminal justice organization and the revolution, and finally the duties and powers of the prosecutor were handed over to the presidents of the courts and the head of the relevant judicial district.

With the problems that this not-so-justified initiative created after the passage of 9 years and the disturbances that appeared in the proceedings, in 1981, with the approval of the law amending the law on the formation of public courts and the revolution, approved in ۲۰۰۷, the judicial system was restored and by article 10 of the amending regulation of this law, the powers of the prosecutor were re-delegated to him.

In this regard, he acted as a competent authority to prosecute crimes, and as stated in article 79 of the law on principles of judicial organizations, major responsibilities were assigned to the prosecutor. At the present time, the prosecutor's office plays an essential and fundamental role in the implementation of criminal justice and the fair and just trial process. The judicial system, as a competent authority, deals with all crimes in the performance of preliminary investigations.

Currently, both deliberate crimes and revolutionary crimes are dealt with in the prosecutor's office, of course, this range includes minor crimes that are punishable by up to 3 months of imprisonment or a fine of up to 1 million rials, or crimes that fall under the category of adultery and adultery, or crimes against children, individuals a minor who is directly presented in court will not be.

Article 156 and article 158 of the constitution states: the duty to detect crime, prosecution, punishment and punishment of criminals, and the implementation of the limits and regulations of the Islamic penal code, and the appropriate action to prevent the occurrence of crime and the reformation of criminals, and the issue of expanding justice and freedoms.

Legitimacy and restoration of public rights is the responsibility of the judiciary. The most suitable organization in this case is the prosecutor's office according to the legal background, the current practice of other countries and past experiences. Considering that article 162 of the constitution explicitly mentions the prosecutor general, this emphasis can be considered as a reason for accepting the prosecution system in the judicial system of the country, in which the prosecutor is responsible for protecting public rights.

In any case, the complete separation of the judicial institution of proceedings (court) from the institution of prosecution and compliance with the principle of independence of the court before the prosecution is contrary to the requirements and necessities of a fair proceeding, and the implementation of the duty of defending the rights of the society requires having the right or duty to supervise the good It is the process of criminal proceedings and appeals against judicial decisions of criminal courts. So, the legislator has expressed his will to actively play the role of the judiciary and the prosecutor, with the attorney general at the head of it. Now, what gaps and complications have arisen in objectifying this will, is a matter that we will deal with later. Below is a list of duties and responsibilities of the prosecutor in the current laws of the country.

The second speech: General duties and responsibilities of the prosecutor in the judicial system in order to pursue and fight against economic crimes

In general, there are 6 chapters for the duties of the prosecutor in the current laws of the country, which are:

- ✓ Prosecutor's duties in criminal matters.
- ✓ Prosecutor's duties in international affairs.
- ✓ Duties of the prosecutor towards the bailiffs in terms of his duty as a bailiff.
- ✓ Duties of the prosecutor in legal matters.
- ✓ Duties of the prosecutor in relation to the duties of organizations and ministries, in terms of monitoring the good implementation of laws.
- ✓ Duties of the prosecutor in special matters

Now, according to the topic of this research, in cases related to economic crimes, it will be briefly discussed and explained.

Paragraph 1: Duties of the prosecutor in criminal matters related to economic crimes

- ✓ The task of detecting crimes, including economic crimes, in the administrative system is the subject of paragraph 3 of the law on the amendment of the law on the formation of public and revolutionary courts.
- ✓ Crime detection through officers headed by the prosecutor.
- ✓ Detecting crimes by reviewing the reports of the inspection organization and other official institutions.
- ✓ Crime detection through public reporting.
- ✓ Detection of crime through the complaint of a private plaintiff.

✓ The duty of prosecuting the accused (filing a lawsuit from the aspect of divine right and protecting public rights).

1- Preliminary research task:

✓ The prosecutor can directly conduct the preliminary investigation of crimes that are not under the jurisdiction of the criminal court.

✓ In crimes that are dealt with by the criminal court of the province, the prosecutor has the right to supervise the investigation conducted by the investigator.

2- The stage of hearing and issuing a verdict:

✓ Appointing a representative to defend the indictment in the general criminal court, revolutionary courts, provincial criminal court and provincial appeals court.

✓ Appealing from court rulings that do not comply with legal standards.

3- The execution stage of the sentence:

✓ Implementation of criminal sentences of general criminal courts, provincial criminal courts, and revolution courts, as well as criminal appeals courts.

✓ Supervision of prisons.

✓ Approval of the offer of conditional release of prisoners.

✓ Offer to pardon the convicts.

✓ Matters related to the criminal record and its supervision.

The second paragraph: Duties and responsibilities of the prosecutor towards the bailiffs in terms of their duties as bailiffs

✓ Supervision and supervision of general and special officers.

✓ Training of officers for their duties.

✓ Issuing cards for officers and organizing them.

The second topic: Introduction of the attorney general and its role in the restoration of public rights in economic crimes

Since our discussion is focused on the attorney general and the restoration of public rights in economic crimes. Therefore, in this speech, we will first explain the background of the position of the attorney general and then explain the duties and legal powers of this institution in the pursuit of economic crimes.

The first speech: Background and coordinates of the general prosecutor's office

As stated earlier, Iran's constitutionalists, by adapting the judicial system after the great french revolution, accepted the judicial system in the various courts, based on which the general prosecutor's office consisting of a prosecutor and an assistant prosecutor along with the courts and tribunals and in order to defend public rights They do their duty.

This law introduced the attorney general as superior to the judicial system and established the necessary organizations to fulfill this role. This establishment as an efficient form and format for the study of criminal justice and the enforcement of public rights was even accepted by the leading constitutional scholars and was not found to be against Sharia.

As article 83 of the constitutional amendment clearly stipulates: The king is responsible for appointing the public prosecutor with the approval of the sharia ruler. In the Law on the principles of judicial organizations approved in 1929, the duty of the public prosecutor was also explained in a way to protect public rights and supervise the implementation of laws and duties according to legal regulations. Before the revolution, the prosecutor's office was under the direct supervision of the country's attorney general, and the state court's prosecutor's office, the provincial court's prosecutor's office, and the city court's office were connected to the country's attorney general and answerable to him through an organic arrangement in a hierarchical system. After the Islamic revolution, until 1968 and before the revision of the constitution, the attorney general of the country was introduced as a member of the Supreme Judicial council and appointed by the leadership in article 162.

At that time, apart from the general prosecutor, the general prosecutor of the revolution, the general military prosecutor, and the special prosecutor general for the clergy were also acting independently and as prosecutors of dedicated courts. With the approach of concentrating the management in the judiciary and removing the doubt, the two-pole system consisting of the head of the supreme court and the prosecutor, both of whom were appointed as leaders, was established in the reforms implemented in the revision of 1990. The attorney general and the president of the supreme court shall be elected under the supervision of the Head of the Judiciary and upon his proposal and the approval of the judges of the supreme court in accordance with the provisions of article 162.

With this establishment, part of the powers of the supreme court president and the attorney general were transferred to the head of the Judiciary. Another issue that was raised in the constitutional review council was the discussion of the attorney general's existential philosophy in article 162 of the constitution.

On the one hand, the title of attorney general was mentioned in two places in the constitution, and on the other hand, with the changes made, it lacked specific responsibilities and duties. If the attorney general was considered a member of the supreme judicial council in the previous constitution, now with the removal of the supreme judicial council, he lost this position and the new constitution did not mention his duties and powers.

Among the terrible complications that happened after the abolition of the prosecutor's offices and still remain today, was the disconnection of the prosecutor's office with the attorney general. At this time, despite the mentality of the people and in accordance with the dignity and objectivity of the attorney general in the legal systems of the world, the attorney general did not have nobility and leadership and supervision over the affairs of the country's prosecutors, so efforts were made to under the banner of centralization and unity of management in the judicial system, this title The constitution should be removed, which of course was not favored by the Judicial commission of the revision Council.

As it was also raised in the 70s, one of the reasons for the opponents of eliminating prosecutors and establishing public courts was the issue of the existence of the attorney general in the constitution. If the attorney general was removed from the constitution, the restoration of the prosecutors would be faced with forms of opposition to the constitution, and in principle, the removal of the prosecutor general from the constitution would be considered as the illegality of the prosecutors.

Another point that was raised in the context of amending article 162 in the revision of 1968 was the issue of adding a number of responsibilities and judicial powers as the duties of the attorney general, which naturally ruled out the possibility of removing it. The responsibilities and powers that the judicial commission proposed for the attorney general were mainly the duties that were not foreseen in the judiciary, such as the restoration of public rights, the expansion of justice and legitimate freedoms, and the prevention of crimes, which are not assigned to a specific agency and no direct person was assigned to perform these roles.

The non-approval of this proposal by the constitutional review council and the relevant judicial commission prompted the council to justify the existence of the attorney general in the constitution with a short sentence, which was that the limits, duties and powers of the attorney general is determined by the law, but this proposal was also not voted and article 162 was only partially changed by the amendment related to concentration.

As mentioned in the current constitution of the country, there is no explicit mention of the judicial system, but article 162 of the constitution mentions the country's attorney general and states how to appoint him. The president of the supreme court and the attorney general must be just and knowledgeable about judicial affairs, and the head of the judiciary, in consultation with the judges of the supreme court, appoints them to this position for a period of 5 years. If you pay attention, the constitution recognizes the existence of the prosecutor's office by naming the person who is at the head of it, but the title of prosecutor general is possible without the prosecutor's office, so the prosecutor's office is rooted in the constitution. Because the constitution, with the provision of the attorney general, has nothing but the establishment of the judicial system and its establishment in the whole country. Otherwise, the establishment of this position as the head office of the country's prosecutor's offices was a futile action without the existence of a prosecutor's office. The evidence shows that the establishment of the prosecutor general's office under the chairmanship of the supreme prosecutor general was considered as a useful experience by the constitutional legislator.

The mention of phrases such as "the head of the prosecutor's office" and "the country's prosecutor's office" in the deliberations of the constitutional experts confirm this. Also, the comparison between the president of the supreme court and the attorney general and the traditional deputy of the prosecutor's office next to the courts seems so obvious that its removal can be considered against the constitution. In any case, the attorney general has been introduced as a high-ranking judicial official in the constitution, and in the current and normal laws of the country, duties and powers have been considered for this high official.

The second speech: Duties and powers of the prosecutor general of the country in economic crimes in the current laws of the country

The institution of the attorney general of the country has experienced three decades of ups and downs and has undergone many changes and developments, so that these developments can be separated into four phases:

- ❖ The position of the attorney general of the country in the constitution from the beginning of the revolution until the date of revision.
- ❖ The position of the attorney general of the country in the constitution from the date of revision until the abolition of the courts.
- ❖ The position of the attorney general of the country in the scope of the abolition of prosecutors.

❖ The position of the attorney general of the country after the revival of
the courts.

❖ Therefore, at the current stage, the duties and responsibilities of the
country's attorney general can be categorized and regulated as follows.

The first paragraph: Duties and responsibilities of the prosecutor general of the country in relation to playing the role of the public prosecutor in economic crimes

With the recognition of the rule of declaring a public crime and separating the divine aspects of crimes from their private aspects in Islamic law, this distinction and separation has also been reflected in the laws of our country, and public lawsuits have found separate coordinates from private lawsuits. Since the mixed system was accepted in the judicial process of our country and the institution of prosecution was separated from the institution of investigation and issuance of sentence, the prosecution was placed under the authority of the court and the issue of pursuing the general aspect of the crime was entrusted to an institution called the public prosecutor's office.

With the drafting of the temporary law on the principles of criminal trials, the rule of declaring a public crime was accepted in our country and was handed over to the prosecutor's office, as stated in article 19 of the criminal procedure code: "The public prosecutor is considered the head of the judiciary, but his special and main mission is prosecution It is a criminal matter. Therefore, in cases where the crime, regardless of the claim for personal loss, is also eligible for public honor and has a public aspect, the public prosecutor must stand up on behalf of the society to restore and fulfill the rights of the people. According to article 50 of the law on principles of judiciary organizations, the public prosecutor was placed at the head of the prosecutor's office, and he was responsible for filing lawsuits and prosecuting crimes from a public perspective.

With the removal of the prosecutor's office from the judicial system in 1995, the duties and powers of the prosecutor were assigned to the presidents of the courts and the head of the relevant judicial district, therefore, article 3 of the law of procedure of the general courts of the revolution had the following provision: General and Islamic boundaries according to legal standards are the responsibility of the head of the judiciary", but after the restoration of the courts in 2003, according to article 10 of the amending regulations of the law on the establishment of public courts and the revolution approved in 2003, these duties were again assigned to the prosecutor. Based on this, the public rights enforcement is the responsibility of the prosecutor, who has been recognized by the legislator as being in charge of prosecution according to his local competence.

It should be mentioned that the attorney general acts as the public prosecutor in the country and the powers of the public prosecutors who act in a field and operational manner in the limited and relevant judicial area cannot be exercised by him, therefore he can prosecute the accused or accused persons from the public prosecutor. place, but it is not allowed to carry out prosecution actions on behalf of the relevant public prosecutor who has the local jurisdiction to prosecute crimes. The guarantee of the implementation of disobedience of the prosecutors from the superior authority in practice can be found in the form of disciplinary prosecution or changing the position and mission of the offending prosecutor by the order of the competent authority.

Based on this, the attorney general of the country, as the public prosecutor in the country, can, in cases where any act or omission in the national arena harms the society and public rights, on behalf of the society, prosecutors who have dignity and operational competence. He wants them to prosecute the aforementioned perpetrators. The attorney general of the country can, according to article 17 of the law amending some of the judicial laws approved in 1987 for the attorney general, and considering article 161 of the constitution and the inquiry of the guardian council regarding the supervision of the supreme court and its judiciary, The legality of proceedings in the courts and courts, as well as the powers of the head of the judiciary to the attorney general of the country to perform the role of the public prosecutor in the country in the best way possible, and if his operational levers are dissatisfied with the tasks assigned by the attorney general, to guarantee its own performance. Therefore, even if the actions or omissions of the officials and officials affiliated with the government and governmental institutions lead to the limitation of the freedom of the society and deprive them of the rights stipulated in the constitution, the attorney general, as the public prosecutor, can take appropriate measures according to article 570 of the Islamic penal code.

The second paragraph: Duties and responsibilities of the prosecutor general of the country in relation to crime prevention, including economic crimes

- ❖ Powers of the head of the Judiciary:
- ❖ Head of the central council of prevention and social protection headquarters: The prevention and social protection headquarters was formed according to the circular of the honorable head of the judiciary. According to this circular, the purpose of forming the headquarters is to revive the cause of good and forbid evil and refer to paragraphs 4 and 5 of article 156 of the constitution and to prevent the occurrence of crime and as prescribed by paragraph 1 of article 158 of the constitution. The head of the judiciary is applied. Among the top members of this staff is the attorney general of the country. As stated in articles 4 and 6 of this directive, the attorney general is the head of the central council, and the secretary of the council is appointed by the selection of the members of the Council and the approval of the Prosecutor, and is responsible for the notification and follow-up of the council's resolutions.

According to article 5 of the guidelines for the establishment of prevention and social protection headquarters, the duties and powers of the central council are as follows:

- ✓ Creating coordination between relevant bodies.
- ✓ Making decisions regarding the general policy and plans of the headquarters.
- ✓ Making a decision regarding the budget and credits of the headquarters within the range that has been allocated.

- ✓ Determining and communicating the duties and responsibilities and organization of provincial units.
- ✓ Supervising the performance of provincial units.
- ✓ Examining and making a decision regarding the received proposals regarding the change and modification of the structure and other communicated matters.
- ✓ Obtaining performance statistics of provincial and city councils.
- ✓ Making a decision on the use of manpower and its lack and quality and determining the ceiling of required posts in the units and within the limits of the available credits and facilities.
- ✓ Creating coordination between relevant organizations such as Naja, Basij, headquarters for good and prohibition of evil, prosecutors, prisons, ministry of Information and other institutions if necessary.
- ✓ Other cases referred by the head of the judiciary.

Of course, it should be noted that by paying attention to the background and the inherent and essential missions of the attorney general of the country, it seems that the task of preventing crime should be concentrated in the institution of the attorney general of the country, and while avoiding parallel work, appropriate arrangements should be considered for this serious task.

- ❖ The head of the headquarters of prevention and fight against special crimes, based on the establishment of prevention headquarters throughout the country, centered on the prosecutor of the provincial capital:
- ❖ Membership in the supreme council for the prevention of crime: According to article 2 of this law, in the implementation of article 156, clause 5 of the constitution, the judiciary must take appropriate action to prevent the occurrence of crime and reform criminals, and adopt comprehensive, coordinated and effective policies in the field of prevention. From crime or the participation of people, local communities and non-governmental organizations, a council called the supreme council

for the prevention of crime is formed under the chairmanship of the head of the judiciary and composed of the following people:

- ✓ First vice president
- ✓ Attorney general of the country
- ✓ Ministers of interior, information, gustice, culture and Islamic guidance, labor and social affairs and education
- ✓ Chairman of the legal and judicial commission of the Islamic council
- ✓ Head of the broadcasting organization
- ✓ Commander of the police force
- ✓ Head of the general inspection organization of the country
- ✓ Vice president of social and crime prevention of the judiciary
- ✓ Head of the judicial organization of the armed forces
- ✓ The head of the organization of prisons and protective and educational measures of the country
- ✓ Head of the center for strategic studies and judicial development
- ✓ Commander of the Basij resistance force
- ✓ Head of the country's welfare organization
- ✓ Secretary of the anti-narcotics headquarters
- ✓ Secretary of Juma imam policy council
- ✓ Chairman of the supreme islamic council of provinces
- ✓ Head of crime prevention organization

Note: Professors, researchers and representatives of other governmental and non-governmental organizations are invited as guest members according to the issues discussed in the council, as determined by the secretary of the council.

According to article 3 of this law, the duties of the crime prevention council are

- ❖ Approval of crime prevention plans and programs.
- ❖ Clarifying the role and duties of each of the government agencies and organizations in the matter of crime prevention within the framework of their legal duties.
- ❖ Adopting appropriate measures in order to coordinate and develop cooperation between the responsible agencies in crime prevention.
- ❖ Examining the bills needed for crime prevention.
- ❖ Appropriate action to amend criminal laws and regulations.
- ❖ Adopting the necessary policies to develop and expand the culture of crime prevention.
- ❖ Taking the necessary measures to attract the participation of people and civil institutions in the preparation, formulation and implementation of crime prevention plans and programs.
- ❖ Evaluating the results of the implementation of plans, programs and the performance of the responsible institutions in the field of crime prevention.
- ❖ Allocation of necessary credits and optimal use of available resources and facilities in the field of crime prevention.

Note 1: Resolutions of this council in the area of the judicial branch's duties are notified by the head of the council after approval by him, and in the area of the executive branch's duties are notified by the president after the approval of the head of the council. After notification, these resolutions are mandatory for all organizations within the scope of their legal duties.

Note 2: The government is obliged to allocate a separate and centralized budget for the implementation of national, regional and local crime prevention programs in the budget line every year.

Article 4 states: In order to monitor the implementation of the supreme council's approvals, help advance national and regional crime prevention policies and programs, and study and research in the strategic areas of crime prevention, a crime prevention organization is established under the supervision of the judiciary with the following duties.:

- ❖ Organizing and monitoring the implementation of national and regional crime prevention plans and programs.
- ❖ Providing regular and periodic reports of the results of the implementation of crime prevention plans and programs to the supreme council.
- ❖ Drafting of crime prevention plans, programs and bills.
- ❖ Examining and identifying criminal laws, regulations, policies and procedures and proposing appropriate action to the supreme council.
- ❖ Assisting organizations in the implementation of policies, programs and approvals of the supreme council for the prevention of crime and efforts to remove the obstacles and problems of its implementation.
- ❖ Studying various forms of delinquency at the national and regional levels.
- ❖ Providing statistics and information needed by the supreme council for crime prevention for policy making.
- ❖ Examining the credits necessary for the implementation of crime prevention plans and programs.
- ❖ Performing the duties of the secretariat of the supreme council for crime prevention.
- ❖ Carrying out other tasks assigned by the supreme council for crime prevention.

Note 1: The head of the organization is the highest executive officer of the organization and is appointed by the decree of the head of the supreme council for crime prevention.

Note 2: In order to deal with the goals and fulfill the assigned tasks, the organization works with the cooperation of the executive bodies to create the necessary specialized organizations and committees. In terms of financial and administrative regulations, this organization is subject to the regulations related to organizations affiliated to the judiciary.

Article 5: This law stipulates: In order to create coordination in the implementation of prevention plans, encourage regional innovations and strengthen local works in this field, the provincial crime prevention council is formed under the chairmanship of the chief Justice of the province and composed of the following people:

- ✓ Governor's political-security deputy.
- ✓ Provincial prosecutor.
- ✓ Chairman of the central Islamic council of the province.
- ✓ The commander of the police district of the province.
- ✓ Director general of prisons and security and disciplinary measures.
- ✓ Director general of education.
- ✓ Director general of Islamic culture and guidance.
- ✓ General manager of labor and social affairs.
- ✓ Director general of radio and television.
- ✓ Director general of the welfare organization.
- ✓ Director general of the provincial information department.
- ✓ Commander of Basij resistance force of the province.
- ✓ Director general of provincial inspection.
- ✓ The head of the judicial organization of the armed forces of the province.

Note 1: Professors, researchers and representatives of other governmental and non-governmental organizations are invited as invited members according to the issues discussed in the council, as determined by the secretary of the council.

Note 2: If necessary, the provincial crime prevention council can initiate the formation of a city crime prevention council under the chairmanship of the chief Justice of the city.

Article 6: The duties of the provincial crime prevention council are

- ✓ Implementation of the approvals and policies of the supreme council of crime policy at the province level.
- ✓ Adopting coordinated provincial measures based on national crime prevention policies.
- ✓ Examining, approving and evaluating provincial and city plans for crime prevention and providing the necessary facilities and platforms for its implementation.
- ✓ Planning to share the views and opinions of citizens and neighborhood residents in the preparation and adjustment of crime prevention programs.
- ✓ Employing and attracting the participation of non-governmental and public institutions in the implementation of crime prevention plans.
- ✓ Providing regular and periodic reports on the implementation of provincial crime prevention plans and programs to the supreme council.
- ✓ Guiding city councils to prevent crime and monitor its performance.

Article 7: By-laws related to the organizations of the crime prevention organization and how the supreme council operates and work methods are prepared by the ministry of justice and approved by the head of the judiciary within three months after the approval of this law. Membership in the supreme council for the prevention of crime in accordance with clause 2, article 2 of the law on the prevention of crime, which was proposed by the judiciary and was discussed and reviewed in the government bills commission and was approved by the Islamic council in the second half of 2007, the prosecutor the whole country is one of the members of the supreme council for the prevention of crime, which is chaired by the head of the judiciary. In the article of this law, it is stated: Crime prevention means: predicting, identifying and evaluating the risk of crime and taking the necessary measures and measures to eliminate or reduce it.

Chapter III

The role of independence of prosecutors in pursuing economic crimes

In this chapter of the book, the role of the independence of prosecutors in pursuing and fighting economic crimes is discussed in two topics.

Topic 1: The independence criteria of the prosecutor

The principle of the independence of prosecutor judges is a single principle in the mind at first, but after careful examination it is divided into partial criteria. In the first speech, an attempt is made to explain and interpret these criteria in detail. In the second speech, the theories related to the separation of powers are examined and researched.

The first speech: definition and explanation of the criteria of independence of prosecutor judges

The prosecutor conducts proceedings to restore injustice and to compensate for oppression and violation, but in order to do justice, the prosecutor must have judicial independence. Many of the jurists and basically the authors of the books of fundamental rights, investigate judicial independence impartially, judging and not prohibiting the removal of a judge from his position and position except in case of violation and trial in a special court and prohibiting the transfer and change of a judge's job. Except in the cases prescribed by the law, they have defined it. The criteria and mechanisms that fall under the general principle of prosecutor's judicial independence are:

- ❖ The criterion of lack of influence and effectiveness of the prosecutor.
- ❖ Criterion prohibiting dismissal of prosecutor judges.
- ❖ The criterion of prohibiting the transfer and change of prosecutor judges.
- ❖ Financial ability of prosecutor judges.
- ❖ The duties and responsibilities of prosecutor judges in maintaining their judicial independence.

The first paragraph: The criterion of non-infiltration and effectiveness of fictional judges:

Regardless of the spiritual and moral dangers that always lie in wait for fictional judges and may lead them to the abyss of destruction, material and social dangers also threaten every judicial system. The powerful and influential people of the society, if you see yourself among the condemned, they will not sit idle to protect their interests and use all their abilities in the form of authority, influence, connections, threats and even bribery. Public institutions, especially the executive branch, stand in front of the judiciary by promoting public interests and do not empower it. Organizational hierarchy is also one of the things that can disrupt the prosecutor's judicial duties and divert the justice. So, it is possible that three different groups infiltrated the work of the prosecutor and had a major impact on it.

- ❖ Haters of society.
- ❖ Executive branch.
- ❖ The appointees of prosecutors, i.e., those who are higher than prosecutor judges and prosecutors in terms of administrative hierarchy.

Judicial security requires that the prosecution judges are independent and immune in terms of their position and lack of influence. The lack of influence means that the prosecution judges do not obey anything but the law in performing their duties and do not interfere with the personal circumstances of the litigants in any way and it doesn't work and their only guide is the court regulations.

Therefore, the principle of non-influence and influence requires that the prosecutor does not have any other job, even administrative, in order not to be influenced in terms of hierarchy. Another main factor that closes the way to influence and influence the story is the spirit of courage and bravery that should not be removed from the story, and the most important factor that can make the principle of judicial independence more practical is the effort to convince the society to respect the principle of judicial independence.

The story is about society's respect for prosecutor judges and their reliance on public opinion so that they can do their work with confidence.

The second paragraph: the criteria for prohibiting the dismissal of prosecutor judges:

Before examining the principle of prohibiting the dismissal of prosecutors and its exceptions, first the methods of selecting and appointing judges, including prosecutor judges, in some countries are examined, because the appointing authority The perpetrator may have an effect on the dismissal. Basically, there are different ways to choose judges.

Selection of judges, including prosecutors, by the people themselves: in line with the theory of those who consider the judiciary to be separate from the other two branches, they choose judges in a free election just as they participate in the elections of representatives of the legislative branch.

This system was first used in France. The number of people and revolutionaries was the rule of the people in all fields, which was abandoned later. Currently, it is common in several cantons of Switzerland and several states of the United States. Currently, it is extremely little implemented, because being a prosecutor is a very technical job, and being a prosecutor judge requires a lot of work and experience in addition to legal knowledge, mental health, and piety. While the situation of being chosen by the people is often political views and pressures of the parties to choose the desired judges. Although such a method may lead to the independence of judges in front of the agents of other powers, but in order to be elected in the next periods, judges think of gaining popularity with voters who are mostly common people, and it is possible that it is a professional policy that lacks judicial authority. is to rely on the masnad Qadha.

Election by the Legislature: To avoid the dangers of electing judges directly by the people, some have suggested the method of electing them by the representatives of the legislature, who are themselves elected by the people. There may be criticisms of this method.

- ✓ **First:** The independence of the powers is impaired.
- ✓ **Second:** There are categories in the parliament and political tendencies are involved in their selection.

Method of appointment: according to the theories of some scholars, the power to choose and install judges can be in the power of the executive branch, and most of the time it is in the hands of the country's presidency or a specific judicial body or elected judges. For example, in France and America, judges are chosen by the president. At the end of the appointment discussion, the selection of judges should be linked to the appointment and sufficient selection with his dismissal. Basically, any office that appoints a person or office holder will have the right to dismiss him. In public power institutions, dismissal and removal of officials is considered as a monitoring tool in management.

Because in some cases, the good course of affairs and some policies require such a decision, but the criterion of inadmissibility of judges, which has the same goal of correct service and execution of justice with its own wisdom, is stable. It is different from the way of dismissing other people in other forces. According to this principle, no authority, even the appointing authority, has the right to dismiss or dismiss judges, except in the cases provided by law, and it is only according to special police procedures and proof of a judge's violation or guilt that the relevant authority has the right to dismiss him.

Different opinions about the dismissal of a judge have been presented in Mobin Islam. A group like Allamah Hali in the Book of Sharayh believes that there is no obstacle to the removal of a judge without the direction of a judge. Because the judge appointed by the imam and head of religion is the deputy and attorney in the judgment, and the client can dismiss his attorney whenever he wants, but another group argued that there is no reason to dismiss the judge without reason and said that judging is a type of guardianship and leadership is in the field of rulings that has been confirmed by the imam for a person. On the other hand, dismissal without a reason is pointless.

Jurists such as Shahid have presented this opinion. It seems that the second theory is more logical and is actually the theory of the majority, and the jurists of the assembly of experts of the Islamic republic of Iran constitution approved in 1980 have accepted this opinion. The rule prohibiting the dismissal of judges, including prosecutors, should not be considered as an absolute rule. This principle also has exceptions an important exception is the dismissal of the prosecutor due to occupational violations or acts and behavior that may be recognized as a crime according to the laws of the respective country. It is only in this case that the prosecuting authority will have the right to dismiss him and prevent him from continuing his service after a full investigation and after proving a police violation or finding him guilty.

Third paragraph: Prohibition criteria for changing and transferring prosecutor judges

This criterion means that prosecutor judges cannot be transferred from one place to another without their will and their place of service can be changed or their judicial job can be turned into an administrative one. The prosecutor or assistant prosecutor must be free in making judgments and decisions, and one of the factors that may affect his independence is changing his position or transferring him from one place to another, and it also causes the violation of people's rights and the slowness of the process of investigation and renewal of time.

Because due to the lack of such a principle, it is possible that the prosecutor or assistant judge not only does not pay attention to the rights of the people due to the lack of job stability and the provision of a place of service, but it is possible that he participates in the cruel thing because of his fear of his future career. The change and transfer of judges may deprive him and his family of personal peace, or influential persons may cause the transfer and, as a result, the impossibility of hearing and issuing judgments regarding the case in question. This principle also has flaws, including the fact that prohibiting the absolute change of judges is against the public interest and may cause corruption. In any case, this rule is necessary to guarantee the job of the prosecutor or assistant prosecutor, his peace of mind and the accurate execution of justice.

The fourth paragraph: Financial ability of prosecutors or prosecutors

The discussion of the judge's salary from the treasury is at the top of the established principles of judgment in Islam, which we come across in jurisprudence texts. According to the opinion of many jurists, such as Bait Al-Mal should be used in the interests of the Muslim community, even if it is obligatory for someone to judge, it does not remove his judicial act from the interests of Muslims, and the tenure of such a person who judges is in the interests of Muslims.

Therefore, he can use Bait Al-Mal. On the other hand, in Islam, it is forbidden to take wages from enemies and it is considered as bribery. Returning sufficient salaries to judges and their financial ability is one of the main factors of maintaining their judicial independence. Therefore, the failure to provide a living wage for a fictional judge may weaken the freedom, independence, and impartiality and, as a result, weaken the role of the prosecutor in the pursuit of economic crimes. The prosecutor, who should follow only the law and a sound conscience, must remain immune from the opinion and taste, and sometimes the threat, greed and taste of the persons and authorities, in order to preserve the dignity of the prosecutor.

The fifth paragraph: Duties and responsibilities of prosecutor judges in maintaining their judicial independence

What helps the independence of the prosecutor more than all the aforementioned criteria is the prosecutor himself. Basically, if there are privileges for the prosecutor in the laws and regulations, then it is about duties and responsibilities. Therefore, he must act according to the principles and regulations specified in the law and use his judicial independence, which is his duty, to serve the people.

The second speech: The role of separation of powers theory in pursuing and fighting economic crimes in the administrative system

This theory is considered the most famous tool of power limitation. The intellectual basis of the inventors of this theory, like other thinkers in favor of the constitutional government, is that a person with power is constantly tempted to abuse it.

The boundless power of arbitrariness is the source of all kinds of corruption and deviations. According to Lord Acton: "Power corrupts and absolute power inevitably corrupts". It is also stated in the wise book of Kalileh and Demeneh: "Whoever sees that his hand is absolute, let his heart be bent on the creation of the world", but in our opinion, accepting the above words absolutely is far from right. Because historical experiences show that power, even absolute power, has not always caused corruption and destruction, and as evidenced by history, the absolute power of prophets such as Prophet Solomon, as well as the political power of the Holy Prophet and his successor Ali, not only caused the expansion of corruption and destruction. It did not happen in society, but it caused a thought-provoking change in its environment and in the following times.

In this way, it seems that what causes the corruption of human power, according to the interpretation of the Holy Qur'an, istighan means to see oneself as needless. In addition to the above, the bitter historical experiences of mankind about the visible wheat of Jo Frosh and those who ate the world under the guise of religion and what slogans they used to say in the interpretation of the Qur'an and said: they had no practical commitment, has caused mankind to seek to invent tools control of power and its renewal, and the weaker morality and spirituality in societies, the more obvious the need to use monitoring and control methods, but anyway, it seems that man-made methods and solutions no matter how much even if it advances, it will not be able to control a society in which people do not believe in moral and spiritual foundations and high human values, and as the holy quran has repeatedly mentioned, such a society will not have a destiny other than destruction and corruption.

This is precisely the reason why most of the western thinkers today consider the existence of people who understand human values and want to achieve them to be the basis for the realization of democracy in practice. Of course, in such a society where most people adhere to values, the solutions presented in political and legal ideas can be effective in preventing the aggression of wrongdoing people, otherwise these ideas will not go anywhere. History is also a good witness for the above claim.

In ancient Rome, when the dangers and internal disruptions threatened the existence and existence of the society, the senate granted one of the consuls as a dictator the choice of absolute and complete powers to prevent the collapse of the social order. He even gave him the right of life and death in the middle, or he issued an order and forced all the men and officials to obey him without question. In the modern world, it is sometimes seen as a solution, such as article 38 of the constitution or article 16 of the constitution of the fifth republic of france.

The distinguishing characteristic of the concept of separation of powers is its emphasis on the abstract concept of separate government institutions, powers, and special tasks. In other words, the conception of the concept of separation of powers requires that in the government, separate areas and special tasks be imagined. Greek thought, due to the lack of access to the concept of separation of powers as it is considered today, is alien, and therefore, the concept of separation of powers should be considered the achievement of the 17th and 18th centuries AD.

Because in the thought of the Greeks, the law was a relatively static and stable phenomenon, and based on the need for the concept of legislative power or flexible executive power, it was not felt. In this way, the judicial power was not separated from the government process in any way. The idea of a composite constitution in Greek thought focused more on the powers of classes and groups within the society, not separate abstract powers, that is, in the discussion of the composite constitution, thinkers were more focused on creating a balance in the ruling elements and wanted the participation of princes, supervisors and elders. were in power. Therefore, they said that the limitation of power was necessary to prevent the abuse of power. However, the balance of governmental powers was considered necessary to guarantee the continuation of the limitation of power.

The concept of distinct functions of the government emerged when the idea of the possibility of law making by humans was accepted and it was here that the separation of law making and law enforcement came to mind. In this era, i.e., in the 17th century, the judiciary was still considered under the executive branch.

Of course, Oliver Cromwell, who took over the government in England at the head of the Persian revolution in the 17th century, was actually very interested in the separation of the legislature from the executive and the balancing power of the judiciary, and he defended the separation of powers in his style and taste, but then after the fall of his government and the re-establishment of the royal system, his ideas were forgotten. John Locke, an English philosopher and thinker in the late 17th century, identified and distinguished three powers in society:

- ✓ Legislature
- ✓ executive branch
- ✓ United Power (Federal).

In his opinion, it is the legislative branch that has the right to use the power of the republic as it wishes and to preserve and protect the society. Laws should be constantly enforced and their force of action should be continuous, while their enactment should be done in a short period of time. So, it is not necessary that this power has been working continuously.

On the other hand, since man is a weak creature, if those who have the power to legislate also have the power to implement it, they will be tempted to abuse the power. Therefore, they either refuse to obey the self-made laws or they mistake them for private profit in the stage of establishment or implementation, and as a result, they think of interests other than the interests of the society's members during the purpose of the society and the government.

Thus, the legislative and executive powers are often separated from each other. Based on his anthropological point of view and the possibility of separating legislative and executive duties from each other and expressing their dangers, he proposes the separation of these two powers from each other. Despite this, he believes that separation and complete independence will cause disorder and loss, and the cooperation of these two forces is mandatory. In accordance with the common thought in England, he considers the legislature to be the sole manifestation of sovereignty, and considers the executive to be accountable to the legislature, and the executive also participates in legislation in a different way.

From his point of view, the united power is responsible for declaring war, making peace and concluding international agreements, and in fact, this power is considered responsible for maintaining the security and interests of society in relation to other countries. In his works, the judiciary is generally not considered an independent power. Because he considers the duty of the judiciary to be outside the political and governmental function.

Despite this, it should be noted that although the identification of the judiciary and its independence against other powers has not been discussed, there has been a defense of the independence of judges since the 16th century, but the emergence of a special independent judicial work is a product of the 18th century. The principle of separation of powers, as it has become popular in the west and most countries of the world today, is the achievement of the French 18th century thinker and philosopher montescu.

He explained the theory of separation of powers in the book ruh al-quwanin and developed his theory around the axis of political freedom. From the design of the above theory, he pursues the attainment of freedom and its preservation, and the basis of his thought is that the human experience tells the abuse of power by humans. Because every person with power tends to abuse his power. Therefore, he rushes forward until he meets a limit, even virtue needs limits from his point of view. In his opinion, freedom emerges and is preserved in moderate governments where the territory and performance of the power holders are limited so that they cannot abuse it.

He writes about the separation of powers: There are three types of power in every government-country: legislative power, executive power for issues related to international law, and executive power for civil affairs. The governor or ruler, through the first power, enacts temporary or permanent laws and cancels or amends the previous laws, and through the second power establishes war or peace, sends or accepts ambassadors, and establishes security and prevents the attacks and by means of the third power, punishes the crime and judges the disputes between the people. Montesquieu considers the community of three powers as the basis for the occurrence of autocracy and the decline of freedom, and he believes that in order to prevent the abuse of power, the governing bodies must be set up in such a way as to stop the power. It is interesting that Mention does not consider the judiciary to have a governmental and political role. Basically, there are two main opinions about the separation of powers:

1- Absolute separation of powers: In this view, the separation of powers is synonymous with the complete independence of the powers from each other and they believe that it is possible to defend the freedom and security of citizens under the shadow of a moderate government. A government in which the legislator does not interfere in the executive affairs and the executive branch has nothing to do with the legislator. According to this group, the balance of powers is possible when the powers are separated from each other by impenetrable walls. Proponents of this view set a certain limit for each of the forces and considered their interference in each other's work as distasteful. In this way, the aforementioned group considered the horizontal separation of powers, in the sense that they assumed the powers to be the same in terms of rank and did not accept their obedience to each other, and they cited the presidential regime as a clear example of the absolute separation of powers, which does not seem very correct.

2- Relative separation of powers: In contrast to the above group, some other jurists believe that the separation of powers is neither scientific nor expedient. To say that political power and sovereignty have a single nature and the exercise of sovereignty in the cooperation group is different manifestations of this sovereignty. Separation of powers is an abstract concept that has been formed based on the abstraction of various special functions of the government, and in practice, it is not possible to determine a precise and clear boundary between pure executive acts and pure legislative acts. The governmental forces must take steps towards completing each other's duties, and interest also requires that the lines of communication between the forces be designed with delicacy and precision. A clear example of separation of powers can be seen in the parliamentary regime. Today, in most countries, they accept and practice the relative separation of powers. Therefore, based on this perception, in the last chapter, we will examine the independence of the judiciary from the perspective of its interaction with the other two branches.

The second topic: Responsibility, immunity and prosecution of judges

In order to ensure the judicial independence of judges, criteria were discussed in the previous discussions, one of which is the duties and responsibilities of the judges themselves in maintaining their independence. This means that the above-mentioned principle must be guaranteed in the laws and regulations, and to prevent judges from abusing their judicial independence, a duty has been recognized for them. In this section, the responsibilities of judges and the definitions of each of them are discussed first, and then the violations of judges, which are listed in the written laws, are stated, and in the last chapter, the discussion of police prosecution of judges, which is actually one of the exceptions to the criteria for dismissing judges, is discussed.

The first speech: Responsibility and immunity of judges

From a literal point of view, responsible means someone who is responsible for a hypothesis that if he does not act, he will be called to account, and responsibility means being responsible and being obliged to do it. In legal terminology, responsibility means a person's legal obligation to remedy the harm he has caused to another. In principle, judges, like other employees, have responsibilities in addition to their legal powers, and in performing their duties, they are responsible for answering their violations, and a special authority is allowed to prosecute and punish them.

In the french legal system, the independence of the judge has been accepted as an absolute and inviolable principle, so that the president himself is obliged to guarantee it. Article 64 of the french constitution stipulates in this regard: "The president is the guarantor of the independence of the judiciary, and the supreme judicial council assists him in this matter, and sitting judges cannot be dismissed." The constitutional council, which, according to the fifty-sixth article of the french constitution, supervises the smooth process of the election of the president and parliamentarians, while emphasizing the impossibility of removal and transfer of judges, has clarified that this is not a personal privilege for judges, but it has been established in order to protect their independence, on which individual freedoms depend.

First paragraph: Criminal liability of judges and their immunity

The concept of responsibility includes criminal responsibility and civil responsibility. Criminal responsibility is caused by crime. Definitions of criminal liability have been made. Criminal liability is a kind of personal obligation to answer for the effects and adverse results of a criminal or criminal phenomenon. Therefore, in any case where a person does or refrains from doing something that is a crime, and with this act, he is exposed to the body, life, freedom, dignity, or property of another person, or if he disturbs the order of the society, he is required to compensate the damage.

Of course, this damage has a general meaning and consists of two parts, firstly, compensation for the material and moral damage of the victim and secondly, suffering the punishment that the society has prescribed as compensation for the violation of its rights. A judge, as a member of the society, may be accused or commit an act or omission for which punishment is prescribed by law, for which he is required to answer for his actions.

Of course, due to the sensitivity and importance of their job, when judges commit a crime, legal regulations cannot be applied to them like ordinary people, but their prosecution and trial must be done under certain conditions and criteria. The purpose of identifying these advantages and immunities is actually to ensure the good performance of job duties and to give security to the relevant job. Criminal immunity is not explicitly mentioned in the basic rights of our country.

Article 164 of the constitution of the Islamic republic of Iran mostly deals with the professional immunity of judges, but it has normal laws and regulations indicating the criminal immunity of judges. According to article 3 of the law on police trial approved in 1307, in cases where the complaints alleging that judicial employees have committed misdemeanors or crimes, or during administrative investigations, it is discovered that the employee in question has committed a misdemeanor or a crime, and the public prosecutor is responsible for that. Find reasons and evidence that require criminal prosecution, request the suspension of the said employee from his job until the issuance of the final decision of the criminal authorities from the police court, and the police trial after considering the reasons and agreeing with the public prosecutor, will order the suspension of the suspect employee. In case of acquittal, the days of suspension will be considered as part of the official service period and will be given to the employee as determined by the government. Another law was the legal bill for the organization of the judges' police court. According to article 11 of this law, whenever it is discovered during the preliminary investigation that a judicial employee has committed a misdemeanor or a crime, and the prosecutor of the police prosecutor's office of the judges considers the reason and evidence that warrants criminal prosecution, suspend the suspect employee from his job.

Until the final verdict of the criminal authorities, the judges will be requested from the police court, and the police court, after examining the reasons and the prosecutor's agreement, will order the suspension of the suspect's employee, and in case of acquittal, it will suspend the suspect's employee for a few days, and if the acquittal is rejected, the suspension will be suspended. It is considered an official service and its provision will be given to the employee.

Therefore, observing the prescribed procedures regarding the removal of judicial immunity from the high police court, which is the issuance of a temporary suspension order from the judicial position, is one of the rules of procedure and is intended to preserve judicial affairs and respect the authority of the judiciary. This method is absolutely necessary to protect judicial independence and ensure their freedom in judicial decisions.

Second paragraph: Civil responsibility of prosecutor judges and their immunity Islamic law has long accepted the principle of responsibility based on fault and the principle of responsibility of the state and society in the course of judicial justice by prescribing the payment of damages by the guilty party in the case of proof of fault and also by Bait Al-Mal in the case of exculpation of fault. In relation to neutrality and avoiding biased actions in the matter of justice, his Islamic rights have a decisive importance.

As he says about David: David, we made you caliph, so judge between people with truth and justice. Also, if the mistake of the judge in the ruling that he issued becomes clear, the ruling is overturned, and if the ruling is followed and the judge is not guilty and the said ruling is about murder or amputation, the ransom is the responsibility of the Muslim treasury, otherwise the judge himself is responsible and he must compensate. Sheikh Muhammad bin Hassan Hur Ameli in the authoritative book Sahil Shia has narrated a narration from Imam Baqir in such a way that if the judges make a mistake at the time of execution or murder, the ransom is paid from the treasury. In Shia and sunni jurisprudence books, there are similar points and narrations regarding the responsibility of the judge, which are limited to the above few points in order to avoid prolonging the words.

The civil responsibility of the judge is based on two jurisprudential rules of non-harm, i.e., whoever causes damage to another, he must compensate, and the second is the rule of tasbib, which is the cause and agent of the damage and is required to repair the damage caused.

In contrast to the rights and privileges that have been considered by the legislator for judges, duties and responsibilities have also been stated. In this case, the judgments issued by the courts must be justified and documented by legal materials, but it is possible that the judges may make a mistake or make a mistake during the hearing of the cases in the matter or in the judgment or in applying the judgment to a specific matter and cause the occurrence of damages and material and spiritual losses will be on the claimants. Is the judge responsible in this case as well, and in fact, moral or charitable responsibility, the person of the judge is not the guarantor?

Basically, the civil responsibility of judges is directly related to the principle of their impartiality, and the issue of observing or not observing impartiality has a decisive role in the way of civil responsibility of judges in the laws of Iran and other countries.

Basically, because of their professional training, religious backgrounds, and professional affairs, judges are less likely to consciously try to violate people's rights. Therefore, most of the losses of judges are the result of mistakes and errors that follow the complexity and heaviness of their work as judges, which are devoid of any malicious intentions. The principle of non-responsibility of the government was considered one of the results of governance until the first half of the 19th century, and it was with the growth of democracy and the emergence of people's rights that its meaning changed and the responsibility of the government towards the people was formed. In Iran, in 1961, the law of civil responsibility was approved, and thus the responsibility of the government and judicial authorities became subject to the general provisions of civil responsibility.

According to article 171 of the constitution of the Islamic republic of Iran, "whenever, due to the fault or mistake of the judge in the matter or in the implementation of the verdict on a particular case, material or moral damage is caused to someone, in case of fault, the guilty party is the guarantor according to Islamic standards, and otherwise the damage will be compensated by the government. According to the mentioned principle, if the judges are found guilty in applying the laws, they will be the guarantor and responsible for the compensation of the damages.

According to article 1 of the civil liability law approved in 1961, anyone without legal permission intentionally or as a result of carelessness causes damage to life or health or property or freedom or dignity or commercial reputation or any other right created for individuals by law. that causes material or moral damage to another, he is responsible for compensation for the damage caused by his act" and according to article 11 of the same law, "government and municipal employees and their affiliated institutions who, on the occasion of performing their duty mainly or as a result of carelessness, cause damage they are personally responsible for the damages, but if the damage is not documented by their actions and is related to the defects of the equipment of the said departments and institutions, in this case, compensation for the damage is the responsibility of the relevant departments and institutions.

The question that is raised in the present discussion is, which authority is competent to establish the fault of the judge, based on which the civil liability of the judge arises? In this regard, the existing regulations do not have the necessary clarity. Regarding the lack of competence of the judge, article 1 of the law on the establishment of the judges' disciplinary court stipulates: "If the head of the judiciary deems the working judge to be incompetent to hold a judicial office according to Sharia standards, he can refer the matter to an expert commission composed of judges, disciplinary prosecutors, The legal deputy of the ministry of Justice and the judicial deputy of the attorney general of the country should refer it for review.

After conducting the investigation, the expert commission will report the result of the matter to the high disciplinary court of Judges to make a decision. The approval of these regulations along with the regulations related to the establishment of the Judges' disciplinary court, which is still legally valid, raises the doubt that due to the recent approval of the judges' disciplinary court, the competent authority to determine the judge's guilt is the same authority, but considering It seems to the mandatory presence of the head of the judiciary in the decisions of the disciplinary court of judges, the legal authority to determine the fault of the prosecutor judge is still the supreme disciplinary court of judges, and the disciplinary court of judges actually acts only as a disciplinary commission.

Now let's see what role the plaintiff has in initiating a lawsuit against the offending judge in the authority where the fault of the judge must be established. Previously, article 2 of the amendment law on the organization of Justice approved in 1957 stipulated: that the high disciplinary court of judges is obliged to hear and rule upon the request of the disciplinary prosecutor or upon the request of the minister of

Justice or the direct complaint of the litigants regarding the violations of all judicial employees in whatever capacity they may be. but later, in the amendment of the aforementioned regulations, by removing the phrase "direct complaint of the litigants" from the text of the law, the judge who suffered from the violation was removed from the number of those who could directly cause the proceedings of the supreme court, even according to the amendment in some cases, despite the conviction of the judge, his criminal prosecution may be suspended.

The second paragraph of article 26 of the law on the amendment of some of the judicial laws has stipulated in this case: that the disciplinary prosecutor of judges can, despite the conviction of a violation by the judge, according to the length of his experience and the amount of his judicial experience, also taking into account his good record and the degree of the judge's interest in performing the assigned duties and the circumstances of the case, suspend his disciplinary action and inform him of the situation.

Therefore, judges may also cause damages to people while performing their duties, which is either due to the judge's fault or negligence in performing legal duties. Fault and negligence are two words that have definitions in law and jurisprudence. In the terminology of law, it is stated in the explanation of the concept of fault that fault is the refusal to do an action despite the ability to do it, and in jurisprudence it is often said to do that action. Also, negligence has been defined in such a way that it is used in contrast to fault and it means: leaving a mandatory law without making any concessions in it, leaving a legal matter or obeying a legal prohibition.

The civil law defines fault in article 953 as follows: "Fault is both negligence and violation". In the definition of trespassing and trespassing in the same law, it is stated: "trespassing is transgressing the limits of permission or convention in relation to another's property or right, and trespassing is the omission of an act that is required by contract or convention to preserve property."

On the other hand, article 1 of the civil responsibilities law approved in 1961 stipulates: Anyone who, without legal permission, intentionally or as a result of carelessness, harms life or health or property or freedom or prestige or commercial reputation or any other right created for individuals by law. If he causes damage that causes material or moral damage to others, he is responsible for compensation for the damage caused by his own actions.

Also, according to article 11 of the law, the government and municipal employees and their affiliated institutions who cause damage to individuals intentionally or as a result of carelessness, are personally responsible for compensation for the damage caused. Considering the above, it seems that the fault is both intentional and unintentional. Therefore, carelessness, carelessness, and non-observance of systems, all of which are unintentional, are included in the category of fault, and the guilty person is also responsible for compensation for the damage caused to people according to the above-mentioned laws.

Article 171 regarding the civil responsibility of judge's states that if a judge causes damage to someone due to his own fault, he is the guarantor, and in case of his mistake, the government is the guarantor. Therefore, the legislator's intention of fault is intentional fault, in which case the prosecuting judge has no immunity and is responsible for compensating the damage, and cases such as mistakes, recklessness, and carelessness that are unintentional are included in the subcategory of negligence, which in this regard due to the job and dangerous situation of a judge, if a judge causes damage to others, since no damage should be left uncompensated, the Islamic state is the guarantor of its compensation, and in fact, judges are immune in these cases, but in cases of fault that the wrongdoer has an intention, the prosecutor's judge is the guarantor of compensation for material and spiritual loss and loss of profit.

The second paragraph: civil responsibility of judges in French law

The French legislator, like other legislators, in order to protect the independence of the judge, for a long time resisted the responsibility of recognizing the judge, especially the government judge, which was objected to by many jurists. Until finally, in 1997, by amending the regulations related to public responsibility, the French legislator accepted the civil responsibility of all judges, including state judges, which later expanded with the formation of the union of European countries, especially the European union, and today the damage caused to citizens is mainly It is compensated by the French government itself.

Of course, if the judge's mistake is serious, the government can move the case to the guilty judge. Therefore, even in this case, the government remains as the civil authority in the judgment of the judge. It is noteworthy that even in cases where the action of the judge and the court is approved by the supreme court of France, it is possible that the applicant can refer to the European court of human rights and refer to paragraph 1 of article 6 of the rules governing that court because his plea has not been considered fairly, he demands the condemnation of his respective government to pay the damages.

The second speech: Violations and prosecution of judges

Judges may also commit violations while performing their duties that will not go unanswered. In this chapter, we will examine the violations committed by judges in connection with their legal duties, and then in the last section, we will discuss the police prosecution of judges based on Islamic laws.

The first paragraph: Judges' violations

Judges, because they are related to people's life, property and honor and are the protectors of people's life, property and honor, they must have excellent qualities that can perform their tasks and duties efficiently, but a limited number of judges is also possible. cause violations and leave the sanctity of the law. Therefore, the judiciary needs control and supervision. For this reason, the task of controlling the actions and behavior of judges and punishing the wrongdoers has been entrusted to the prosecutor's office and the high police court of judges. Judges, the existence of such a reference is necessary.

On the other hand, defining the exact boundaries of offenses and violations of police laws strengthens the principle of judicial independence. The first law regarding the police violations of judges and the determination of punishment for all types of offenses was the General Penal Law of 1926, which was foreseen in article 288 of some types of police violations.

Prohibition of prosecuting against the facts, or agreeing to the said order, or the criminal's failure to receive legal punishment, or non-fulfillment of duties by the inspectors, as well as the order of guilt, or agreeing to the said order with the sentence of conviction of an innocent person, in the event that due to tolerance or negligence be in the same way, afraq or unnecessary violence is considered an administrative offense in the punishment. Administrative punishment for the aforementioned offenses and all types of administrative offenses will be carried out according to the regulations of the ministry of Justice.

In 1928, the council of ministers approved a single article regarding one of these violations. Judges who do not fully explain their rulings will be sentenced to the 2nd to 6th grade punishment mentioned in article 38 of the national employment law. In line with the implementation of article 288 of the public punishment law approved in 1926, the council of ministers approved a regulation under the title of two regulations on identifying the faults of judges and determining their punishment, which includes 27 articles. Cases such as non-observance of the formal articles of the law on principles of trials, disorder in the affairs of the branches and court offices, non-observance of court chiefs over the courts and non-observance of the principles of judicial formations, delaying the court session outside of the scheduled time without a valid excuse or without a written request from the litigants.

Disclosure of opinions and judgments before the official announcement of the recording and non-recording of the documents and information provided by the litigants to the court by the judges without observing the relevant laws, absenting the members of the court without a valid excuse, committing acts against the dignity and honor of the judges. All of the above cases are listed as police violations in the aforementioned regulation. During the several years of the court and the supreme police court, judges have been cited by the judges of this court, and the judges punished the violators based on it, but the violations mentioned in other laws are as follows.

- ❖ Membership in political parties and party propaganda, etc.
- ❖ Classification and alliance to shut down the courts.
- ❖ Punishment for delay in collecting the causes and reasons of the crime.
- ❖ Obtaining inappropriate insurance from the supplement.
- ❖ Failure to accept a lawyer by the court.

In addition to the above cases, in the list of other legal rules and regulations, there are cases that non-observance of which is considered as a police violation of the judge. After the victory of the Islamic revolution, the first transformation should take place in the country's judiciary.

For this purpose, in 1979, the legal bill to reform the judicial organization and the law on the employment of judges was approved by the revolutionary council. According to article 1 of this law, for the liquidation of the administrative and judicial organization of the judiciary, a board consisting of 5 judges as main members and two alternate members will be formed upon the proposal of the minister of justice and the approval of the council of ministers. The aforementioned board can dissolve any of the courts and judicial references that it deems necessary, and if necessary, reconstitute them after liquidation.

On March 23, 1979, a legal bill was approved under the title of the legal bill for the dissolution of the supreme court of the country and its prosecution and police courts and police appeals. In this way, the judges' police court was dissolved and a new court was established. In this way, the first police court was created after the victory of the Islamic revolution. Although there have been fundamental changes in the structures and organizations of the prosecutor's office and the high court of justice of judges, the laws and regulations that existed before the revolution regarding the manner of proceedings by the high court, actions, investigations, and the duties and procedures of police prosecution by the prosecutor's office still remain in force. The law of 1335 rules in this regard.

The duties that were the responsibility of the minister of justice were assigned to the high judicial council after the victory of the revolution and to the head of the judiciary after a review, but the most important law that was approved in the field of police prosecution of judges in the system of the Islamic republic of Iran is the law on establishing the police trial of judges.

It was approved on November 23, 1992 in the expediency assembly. Of course, the aforementioned law had a 5-year deadline, which ended in 1997. In 1998, a new law entitled the law on jurisdiction of judges was approved by the Islamic council. This law, which replaced the law on the establishment of the high police court of judges approved in 1997, also has a court that, according to article 1, is responsible for examining the judicial competence whose competence is questioned according to the legal standards of the authorized authorities in this law. The aforementioned court, which is called the supreme police court of judges, will consist of 3 judges of group 8.

It is stipulated in this law; the authority of a judge may be questioned by one of the following authorities.

- ✓ Head of the Judiciary.
- ✓ President of the supreme court of the country.
- ✓ Attorney general of the country.
- ✓ The heads of the branches of the high civil court of judges.
- ✓ Judges, police prosecutors.
- ✓ Head of the national inspection organization.

The head of the judicial organization of the armed forces to the judges of this organization. According to article 3, whenever the authority of the subject of article 2 is questioned by the authorities, the matter is first referred to the expert commission of the composite center of the judicial deputy of the head of the judiciary, the legal deputy and parliament affairs of the ministry of Justice, the judicial deputy of the supreme court of the country, and the police prosecutor of the judges becomes the commission will investigate and report the result to the court within 3 months at most.

Also, according to article 4, if the majority of the court members rule on the incompetence of the accused judge, he will be sentenced to one of the punishments of permanent dismissal from government jobs, permanent dismissal from judicial jobs, repurchase or retirement. It is worth pondering that there may be a mistake in the competence of this authority with the high police court, it seems that the legislator wanted some kind of allocation of duties or division of work.

Because, first of all, both references are mentioned in article 7. Therefore, he signed an institution called the supreme police court and recognized it as a formality alongside the police court. Secondly, carefully in the duties and authority of the high police court, which includes dealing with bad reputation or behavior and acts contrary to dignity and judicial affairs or political deviations, dealing with violations of unjustified absence and disobedience to administrative systems, applying private theories in making judicial decisions and negligence and forgiveness is in the performance of the duty, we will notice that the task of the criminal court is only in dealing with the judicial competence of the judge and this is due to the importance that the Islamic republic of Iran system has given to the matter of justice and having the conditions and attributes of judgment.

Another important issue that is raised in the discussion of the judges' police court is the relationship between the supreme court of the country and this institution. One of the duties of the supreme court of the country is to supervise the work of the courts according to article 161 of the constitution. If the court considers the ruling against the law, it will conduct a formal investigation and either uphold or violate the ruling and refer to another court, considering that the supreme police court of judges is part of the courts of justice, it also has the right to supervise this court. According to the note of the second article of the law on the amendment of the organization of justice and the amendment of a part of the law on the principles of judicial formations, which was approved in 1957, the violations of the president and members of the high police court are dealt with in the general body of the high court of the country.

Therefore, the court as an authority oversees this institution and supervises it, and this itself has a great impact on maintaining the judicial independence of judges.

Chapter IV

Necessary conditions for prosecutors to pursue economic crimes in the administrative system

It was observed that in the first and second chapters, although briefly, the independent prosecution of this institution was discussed in line with the pursuit of economic crimes as one of the important pillars of the administrative system of the society. In this chapter, in three topics, the position of prosecutor judges in the judiciary, the conditions of prosecutor judges in the pursuit of large economic crimes in the administrative system, and finally, the methods of selecting prosecutor judges and its impact on the pursuit of economic crimes are discussed.

Topic 1: The general conditions of the prosecutor's judge in the judicial institution and its impact on the pursuit of economic crimes

The judicial system should do its best to select people who are resistant to the pressure of the influential classes. Because if such persons work in the judiciary as prosecutors, the judiciary will be successful in implementing real justice. In this way, it seems that not everyone is qualified to hold the position of prosecutor and it is necessary for certain persons to be in charge of this position. Because the protection of the value system of every society and the control and follow-up of the crimes of the social powers and the supervision of the implementation of law and justice are entrusted to these people, and in other words, they are the last refuge of the people against the oppression and injustice of the government and directly, the prosecutors. and the poor people of the society who leave such a lofty position in the hands of unworthy people. In this way, the intellectuals of the world agree that if we want to achieve justice, it is necessary for prosecutors to have certain qualities and characteristics. With regard to the aforementioned, we can discuss the attributes and characteristics that should be considered about the prosecutor's judge under two headings.

The first speech: Scientific and specialized characteristics of prosecutor judges

As we will see in the following materials, most countries and legal systems consider the existence of some scientific qualifications in a judge as a condition, but it seems that in the discussion of the scientific and specialized characteristics of prosecutor judges, several points are important and can be discussed in future studies and providing effective and useful practical solutions. First of all, the scientific standards required for the position of prosecutor are a function of the ruler's point of view regarding the role of the prosecutor's judge in judicial decision-making in pursuing or not pursuing economic crimes, especially economic crimes of the powers of society.

For example, in common law legal systems, only the prosecutor's ability to deduce from the law is not considered as the evaluation criterion for prosecutor judges, and the judge's awareness of social sciences is also taken into consideration, but in countries that have codified laws, the nature of the laws and legal system and the philosophy of the background law.

It limits the judge's direct feeling and inspiration to a great extent. In this system, they pay more attention to legal logic than anything else, and court judgments are completely embellished with legal logic so that they appear completely correct in the framework of education and training based on legal logic, although it may be unfair or strange from the point of view of most people in the society show off In short, in such countries, in meeting the conditions of judges, more emphasis is placed on interpretive methods or interpretive logic, and judges' information is measured from this point of view, but in our opinion, according to the analysis we presented of the nature of law, it seems that in the countries of law It is also necessary for prosecutors to understand the social, economic and religious relations well, so that they can recognize the beautiful and charming face of justice and truth among the false decorations of the rich and powerful. In order to achieve this goal, it is appropriate to evaluate and examine the scientific and experimental level of judges in such issues in the selection of judges, especially prosecution judges.

The Islamic system has confirmed the above opinion of Mehr that based on the above-mentioned content, the power in the Islamic system is for the purpose of establishing the right and rejecting the false and establishing justice, and the recognition of the right is the responsibility of those who are ignorant of the requirements of time and place. does not come.

Another point that is significant in determining scientific criteria is the position of the legal education system and the status of law schools and seminaries. Undoubtedly, the scientific level of law schools and the methods of education and the kind of perspective that these scientific centers teach students about the role of law and law in society have a central and decisive position in determining scientific criteria. Today, in different countries of the world, law and law are considered to be a changing matter that changes continuously and quickly, and professors, students, and graduates need to constantly change and coordinate their information and approaches.

Despite this, unfortunately, in our country, despite the importance of legal education and research, especially the legal system that conforms to Islamic standards has been met with indifference and a consistent and continuous movement in this field is not seen. It seems that it is mostly based on the principles of jurisprudence, they should study other interpretative logics more seriously and, in this way, from the experiences of other countries and the methods reflected in the written works of jurists to extract appropriate interpretative methods and formulate a use coherent and synchronized legal logic with the needs of the day.

It is also necessary to define and explain the position of the legal system based on interdisciplinary studies among other social sciences, so that jurists can better understand social, economic and cultural relations, both in the position of proposing and amending laws and in the position of interpreting existing laws based on scientific criteria. In this way, the way to establish and implement laws based on social needs and public interests will be opened.

Hazrat Imam has also pointed out the said defect and the necessity of efforts in this field in several cases: "The Hosahs were not thinking about these issues, that is, the Hohsahs were following the same rulings that are common among themselves and the place where the people suffer. There is no government issue to think about. This has just happened, and the districts are looking for it to train people, and I have ordered a lot and will continue to do so, but this issue is of course difficult. The seminaries, which should be delivered by the judge of all conditions, were hopelessly out of all matters, especially judging.

The efforts of the famous scholars and great jurisprudents were busy with devotional books of jurisprudence and some books of transactions, and they were unable to deliver hundreds of judges, judges of all the laws. It is necessary to shorten the hands of the judges who disregard the rules of Islam and possibly anti-Islam from the diseases and souls of the nation and not delaying the judgment, which causes chaos and attacks on diseases and properties. In contrast to the above, some may refer to the books written under the title of principles of inference or legal logic of Islam as steps in this way, but it seems that such works have several major drawbacks:

First: of all, the contents of the mentioned materials in these books were compiled from Islamic sources for deriving Sharia rulings, while it should be noted that what we use in the derivation of sharia rulings and the interpretation of the meaning of the infallible or God almighty, even assuming that it is useful for deriving rulings from the text of the law, which cannot be compared with Shari'a texts in terms of content validity, and do not have the necessary effectiveness. Therefore, it seems that in this way, the place of law in the social system in general and the place of law in the Islamic system in particular should be determined in order to identify and use the appropriate method of the law.

Secondly: Many of the contents mentioned in these writings are not useful in practice and cause boredom among the young generation and students. Therefore, we consider it appropriate to talk about some of the characteristics of a suitable legal education system and some shortcomings of the current education system and to explain the position of law education in relation to the pursuit of economic crimes by prosecutors.

The first paragraph: The effect of law education in the pursuit of economic crimes in the administrative system

The characteristics of the guardians of social norms and values can largely be considered the product of the country's education system. This means that the human force of the judiciary is trained in the country's education system and acquires the necessary abilities to hold the position of judge or work as a lawyer or notary. In other words, if the legal society and the legal education system of each country are not able to explain the legal norms and values, the justice system officials who arise from the same society and system, at best, will have extremely confused opinions and views, and certainly from such people cannot be expected to create a stable and stable order, and without a doubt, such people cannot act as guardians of justice and accepted values of governance. Therefore, it seems that the stability of the judicial system and the justice system is largely due to the education system of the country. Therefore, in order to explain the role of the said system and provide solutions, we found it appropriate to investigate the educational system under three headings:

A) educational content;

B) Students;

C) Professors;

Although, in addition to the above factors and components, other factors are also influential in the efficiency of the educational system, but due to the avoidance of delaying the discussion, we will focus on the above factors, which are more important than other factors in our opinion, and sometimes we will also make a passing reference to other factors during the discussion.

A) Educational content: As we mentioned many times in the discussions, law education is important in two ways:

- ✓ Introducing social norms and values in the form of laws and regulations and expressing its philosophical, social, cultural and religious foundations.
- ✓ How to apply laws and regulations to control social relations and inspect it.

Based on this, it seems that the content of educational books should be such that it can handle both of the above missions well, in the sense that, in the first place, in addition to teaching the content of laws and regulations, their legitimacy or rationality should also be taught in a favorable manner.

Educational books should be explained so that students believe in the correctness and efficiency of laws and rules and can serve the legal community with inner peace as soldiers of justice. In order to achieve this goal, it is suggested to pay more attention to the philosophical issues of law and jurisprudence and interdisciplinary studies in law so that we are not vulnerable to the wave of modernity and values that sometimes enter the country in the process of economic development. In the next step, students should be taught the method of inferring and applying legal rules in the form of legal logic or interpretation methods and reasoning techniques so that students can find the appropriate rule and efficient way to resolve a lawsuit in legal disputes and problem solving.

Undoubtedly, memorization training in law is rejected. Because the nature of legal work is such that legal information and reservations will not work without developing the power of thinking and analyzing issues. Despite this, unfortunately, the exams that are held to enter judicial professions in Iran, in such a way that it actually has significant contradictions with the educational content discussed above. Because in the entrance exam for judging, lawyering, notary, counseling and even master of law, what is measured is the students' or graduates' qualifications, not their reasoning and thinking power which is the main focus of legal work and unfortunately, in this regard, due to the profitability of each Today, books with the same color and style are published in the market.

At the end of this article, it is important to mention that in advanced countries, in addition to teaching methods of interpretation and reasoning, in order to facilitate access to laws and reduce the time of the process of inferring and extracting legal rulings, the method of codification or preparation of legal codes is used, which is especially Paying attention to the breadth of laws and regulations, both in terms of their volume and in terms of the variety of issues and issues, both in terms of education and in practice, is very useful and opens the way.

B) Students: The selection of students to study law is very important for the government. Because as we said, the purpose of legal education is to prepare forces to maintain the value system and social norms, and certainly if the people who do not accept the value system as the basis of the legal system and seek to gain fame and power, they will harm the society even if they are given the best education and a lot of money is spent on their thinking power, they will not serve the legal system and advance social goals.

Therefore, it is necessary to be extra careful in the selection of law or jurisprudence and fundamentals of law students and students who want to hold judicial positions, so that the social costs do not have an adverse result. In this way, it is recommended that in addition to intellectual and scientific fields, the following factors should be considered:

B1) Interest: Undoubtedly, seeking justice and seeking rights requires that the student is a real seeker and seeker of them, that is, a student who enters the university and the scientific environment for a degree and the like, not only does he slip in the middle of the road, but it also reduces the motivation and desire of others. In his letter to malik, regarding the qualities of a judge, hazrat Ali emphasizes these qualities: a judge should not be satisfied with a little knowledge until he reaches the truth, and should be more patient in his doubts, in his attitude, and be more patient in revealing things.

B2) Capacity and Cultivation: Our ancestors believed that one should be careful in selection and science should not be given to unqualified and low-capacity people. Because such a thing is like putting a razor in the hands of a drunkard, and its consequences will be nothing but harm to the people, and such a person will also destroy himself due to his lack of capacity. Knowing and having knowledge about everything and for everyone is not valid and useful, especially when the learner does not have the capacity for it. Molavi expresses this issue in another place as follows: In this way, it can be seen that an incompetent person, if he becomes aware of some information and knowledge, causes his own destruction and the ruin of the society.

B3) Patience and acceptance of the teacher: As we know, learning science and cultivating the power of thinking requires patience and tolerance and strictness of the teacher. Arrogant and pampered people, even though they have high intelligence, cannot survive in the educational environment, especially if they consider themselves higher than the teacher and, as a result, do not need guidance and study materials. Undoubtedly, these people always aggressively and sometimes rudely seek to show off, while the condition of learning science is humility and the spirit of tolerance of other people's opinions and opinions. In the truly scientific environments of the west, scientists accept and train those who are really interested in science and knowledge as real students. Fascination is also directly related to mastery. A person who considers himself Allamah Dehar and is always thinking whether he is doing harm or benefit here, he will not be fascinated, he does not have love, he thinks materially and only thinks about personal development. An experienced teacher understands this well and quickly and does not accept such people. In other words, the creation and development of an organized scientific system depends on this factor, i.e., acceptance of professors. A coherent system must also grow, and its growth depends on attracting new forces and cultivating them, provided that the new forces are teachable and accept that scientific system internally, and with the companionship and expenditure of force and in a common direction, strength and growth.

increase that system, not that the forces are used in different directions and the results of the forces become zero or negative, as is the case in many scientific circles of Iran. Unfortunately, in Iranian law, the issue of incompetent professors has negatively affected legal education, especially the separation of the judicial system from universities and seminaries, and the mutual negation of the opinions of seminarians and academics, as well as not addressing the roots of science and its foundations in Iran. The escalation of this has a significant effect.

B4) Pride: One of the evils of education is pride, the presence of which among teachers and students causes the deterioration of the educational system. One of the innocents says in this regard: Pride and self-righteousness prevent a person from learning. Pride and self-righteousness not only hinder research, but also destroys the motivation for research and stepping on the hard and uneven path of knowledge among students and professors. Ragheb Esfahani says: Iblis said that there are three situations in which he is found, I have found my need from him, whoever considers his knowledge to be high and forgets his religion and becomes proud and surprised by his opinion.

C) Professors: The persons who, as professors, take on the serious task of educating young people and the human resources needed by the judiciary, must have the characteristics of a real scientist. Especially in the field of law, which is designed to maintain and support the norms derived from the value system, attention to the moral and spiritual aspects of professors is of particular importance. Because professors have an important role in the formation of the social and moral character of students, but in the current situation, due to the excessive expansion of law higher education centers, people are used as professors who lack the necessary specialized knowledge, the ability to think and analyze and build a coherent thought and they are love, interest, perseverance and endurance.

For example, despite the repeated emphasis of the constitution of the Islamic republic of Iran on the agreement of laws and regulations with Islamic rulings or rather, their non-contradiction with Islamic standards, it can be seen that there are professors teaching in universities and law schools who are even able to use jurisprudence sources. and worst of all, due to ignorance of the method of inferring and extracting Islamic rulings and the intellectual paradigm governing the cognitive methodology of Islamic law and the logic of Islamic law with western and sometimes common standards, they criticize Islamic laws and regulations and even they mock that this causes students to mistrust our Islamic and traditional normative system.

Unfortunately, there are not enough and understandable books written for students in the market, which will also undermine the independence of the judiciary. Professors who are familiar with Islamic courses sometimes limit themselves to reading jurisprudence texts and translating them in the classrooms and do not have the ability to reason and convey values correctly and due to their unfamiliarity with new legal systems, they do not have the power to respond to students' problems. Sometimes they negate beneficial human experiences, which also confuses and misleads intelligent students. Therefore, it is necessary to train professors in the system of the Islamic republic of Iran who are both familiar with its new legal systems and who know the Islamic legal system well so that we can pass on our values and norms to the next generation.

The second speech: the moral and personality characteristics of the judge
The need to have moral and spiritual qualifications for judges is something that is accepted by all legal systems and nations. Therefore, due to its improvisation, we refrain from discussing it in detail. In the 10th principle of the basic principles of judicial independence approved in 1985, the persons who are chosen for judicial jobs must adhere to moral and decent principles.
Also, the necessity of judges' moral qualifications is well inferred from the 15th principle. Because according to it, the judges of the courts are required to observe

professional confidentiality regarding negotiations and confidential information obtained in the course of performing their duties, and other than public proceedings, people should not be forced to testify about these matters.

Also, paying attention to ethical issues in swearing an oath to serve as a judge in France has been considered by the legislator. The text of the oath in France is as follows: I swear to perform my duties well and accurately and to keep with great care the secrets that I come to know through negotiation and discussion, and in general to act as a judge. I will behave with respect and integrity. We would like to point out that the importance of swearing in the opinion of the French legislator is to the extent that it has stipulated that any judicial act of the judge without swearing is condemned to be null and void.

From the point of view of Islamic jurists, considering that the position of judging is one of the noble positions that is fixed by God almighty for the prophet, on his behalf for the infallible imams, and on their behalf for the jurist of all the conditions. The possession of moral and spiritual qualifications should be considered with serious attention in the selection of judges, especially since the Imam repeatedly emphasized the importance of the position of the judge and introduced the judges as guardians of the dignity of Islam.

The second issue: the necessary conditions of the prosecutor in the pursuit of economic crimes in the administrative system

The two basic foundations of the independence of the prosecutor's office are formed in the discussion of the selection of judges and their selection methods. It is important to address the necessary conditions for prosecutors in the pursuit of economic crimes in two ways: choosing competent and capable people to advance and realize the desired goals in the prosecutor's office and prevent the exercise of taste and influence in the selection of prosecutors. Below, in order to determine the importance of the discussion with the legislators of different countries, we will examine the mentioned conditions in the countries of England, France and Iran.

The first speech: the terms of a judge and a lawyer in the English legal system

The approved laws of this country in the field of setting up the courts have not mentioned the necessary conditions for holding the office of a judge, but other laws and legal traditions are based on the fact that judges are chosen from among the lawyers involved in the work of legal affairs, and for this purpose, they also have a certain background They know it is necessary. In this way, the necessary conditions for choosing a judge are the same as the necessary conditions for choosing a lawyer. In this way, the presence of the following conditions is necessary to hold the position of judge in Tali courts:

- ✓ Working as a lawyer in legal matters.
- ✓ Continuity of advocacy for a period of at least ten years attached to the judgment.
- ✓ Famous for good character and sufficiency.

In order to hold the position of judge in the high courts, it is also necessary to fulfill the above conditions, but the minimum term of law is fifteen years.

The second speech: the terms of the judge and the lawyer in the French legal system

In France, the employment of judges must have raised some conditions that can be referred to as general conditions and scientific conditions. General conditions have been established in article 16 of the 1958 directive. Among the mentioned conditions, some can be considered as general conditions needed to obtain government jobs. These conditions are:

- ✓ Having French citizenship.
- ✓ Enjoying civil and citizenship rights.
- ✓ Having a good moral status.
- ✓ Proportionate and orderly situation in terms of the conscription service law.
- ✓ Having a suitable and necessary physical condition for the job of judging and physical health.
- ✓ Not having a special disease that leads to the use of long-term leave.

However, regarding the academic requirements, we must note that the candidate for the office of prosecutor judges must present a document that shows that he has completed education for at least four years after the bachelor's degree, but it is necessary to mention two points:

First of all, the legal texts did not consider it necessary to have a master's degree in law and even left the way open for the acceptance of an equivalent degree.

Second, the conditions related to the documents are not universal and sometimes the candidate will be exempted from these conditions, all of which depends on the ways to enter the job of judging, which are many and varied in France.

The third speech: the terms of the prosecutor in Iran's legal system

In the system of the Islamic Republic of Iran, according to the 163rd article of the constitution, the qualities and conditions of the judge are determined by the law according to jurisprudence standards. In this regard, according to the law on the conditions for the selection of judges, which consists of a single article and a note, judges are selected from those who meet the following conditions:

- ✓ Faith and justice and practical commitment to Islamic standards and loyalty to the system of the Islamic republic of Iran.
- ✓ Productive purity.
- ✓ Iranian citizenship and doing military service or having a legal exemption.
- ✓ Good temperament and ability to do work and not addicted to drugs.
- ✓ Having ijtihad as recognized by the supreme judicial council or the permission of the supreme judicial council.

The second topic: obligatory conditions for a judge (prosecutor) in Islamic jurisprudence

A) Public jurisprudence: Jurists differ on the number of conditions necessary to qualify for the post of judge. Mainly and briefly, the necessary conditions for judging are: maturity, intellect, freedom, Islam, masculinity, ijtihad and justice, which we will discuss further.

    A1) Maturity: Popular jurists believe that religious maturity is a basic condition for holding a judgeship. Because non-adults are not subject to

Sharia rules. Jurisprudents have not set a specific age for becoming a judge after reaching maturity, and have considered maturity as the limit of duty and attention. Despite this, in the Islamic system, the age of growth and intellectual maturity has been considered in practice. Hazrat Rasool appointed Atab bin Asaid as the judge of Makkah at the age of twenty and appointed Umar bin Khattab to judge Basra at a young age, and for this reason, Ma'mun Abbasi also chose Yahya bin Aktham to be the judge of Basra, and when they taunted him, in response He wrote to the detractors that Yahya is greater than Atab bin Asaid, who was chosen to judge by the hand of the messenger, and also greater than the martyrs of jabal, who was chosen to judge Yemen during the time of the Messenger of God. Also, he is older than Ka'b big Sur, who was appointed by Umar bin Khattab to judge in Basra.

A2) Intellect: The jurists agree on the conditionality of intellect for holding the office of judge. Because reason is the basis and criterion of duty. What is meant by reason, reason is not a proof of necessity, but reason that is the source of cleanness and correctness, avoiding mistakes and negligence, and solving problems and dilemmas. Researchers believe that judgment requires knowledge, understanding and piety, despite this, most researchers have prioritized understanding over science. Because understanding is the means of acquiring knowledge, negotiating and memorizing material, but the means of understanding is reason, and it is with the help of reason that one can distinguish error from right and truth from falsehood, and move beyond words and follow the movements and indications of facts.

A3) Freedom: Although jurists have discussed freedom in their works, I do not see the need to discuss it due to the abolition of the slavery system in the present age.

A4) Islam: The jurists believe that believing in Islam is a condition for the correctness of assuming the office of judge and the correctness of judicial decisions. Of course, in the assumption that all or some of the people surrounding the lawsuit are Muslims, the followers of different Islamic schools, including Shafi'i, Maliki, Hanbali, Hanafi, and Zahiri consider Islam as a condition. Sunnis believe that judgment requires testimony, and since one of the conditions for testimony is the witness's being a Muslim. Therefore, appointing a non-Muslim to judge is not correct. In this way, there is no doubt that the prohibition of appointing non-Muslim judges and invalidating their judgments among Muslims has a rational and logical justification and is in favor of truth and justice and is compatible with the tolerance and flexibility of Islam. Despite the above content, Sunnis have accepted the judgment of the infidel in times of necessity, such as when the infidels prevail over the Muslims and appoint an infidel to judge among the Muslims.

A5) Masculinity: There is a difference of opinion among the jurists of popular schools of thought regarding the judgment of a woman: Maliki, Shafi'i and Hanbal believe that one of the conditions for a judge is to be male, but the Hanafis believe that maleness is not a valid condition for the appointment of a judge, and although they believe that such appointing is prohibited by Sharia law, and in the case of appointment, the ruling of a female judge is considered to be valid, except for the limits of retribution and their argument is that the testimony of a woman is not acceptable in terms of retribution and retribution, and because qada is based on testimony. Therefore, the woman's judgment in this matter is rejected and has no effect, but Tabari and Ahl al-Zahir, including Ibn Haram al-Andalusi, believe that the woman's judgment is absolutely valid, even in terms of punishment and retribution. Regarding his decision, Haram argues that being a woman does not prevent understanding the subject of the dispute and the reasons of the parties to the dispute and recognizing the truth. Therefore, the woman's judgment is correct. If we consider such an argument sufficient, it seems that all other conditions should be canceled, while the existence of the above conditions is necessary, but not sufficient. In the continuation of his argument, he states that a woman can be a mufti. Therefore, it is not forbidden for him to become a judge. In response to this argument, they have said that the subject of consultation is different from judgment and the above analogy has no correct basis. Because the subject of consultation with the ruling of Sharia is on a specific issue, while in judgment, the judge issues a binding ruling and the issue of guardianship is raised in it.

A6) Ijtihad: Ijtihad in the word means putting forth effort and ignorance, and it requires hard work, but Ijtihad in the term is: a person's ability to derive rulings from sharia sources. In other words, the condition of ijtihad indicates the need for scientific qualification to attain the position of judge. Sunnis consider four conditions necessary for ijtihad:

- ✓ Knowledge of the book of Allah and knowledge of its rulings in terms of abrogation and abrogation, firm and similar.
- ✓ Knowledge of the sunnah of the holy prophet, both oral and current, and knowledge of all types of hadiths.
- ✓ Knowledge of the opinions and sayings of the past to know the positions of consensus.
- ✓ Science by analogy in order to reject the tacit branches into the spoken and consensus branches.

Basically, there are two sayings among Sunnis about whether or not ijtihad is a condition for a judge:

Shafi'i, Hanbali and Zahiri believe that the judge must be a mujtahid and the judgment of a non-mujtahid is not valid. A group of Malikiya and Hanafiya also believe in this, and another group of Malikiya and Hanafiya believe that ijtihad is not a condition for the validity of holding the office of judge, but this condition is a condition of perfection and priority. Therefore, his opinion is based on the fact that the goal and purpose of judging is the season of hostility and obtaining justice from the oppressor, which is also the responsibility of a non-mujtahid. Because a person can benefit from the knowledge of his mujtahid or scientific leader, but despite this, they have said that it is not permissible to imitate such a person. Because his corruption is more than his goodness and he rule unjustly without realizing it.

A7) Justice: A group of Sunni writers have said in the definition of justice that justice consists of: that the candidate for judgment is truthful, faithful and chaste towards forbidden things and pious against sins and away from doubt and that people are safe from his wrath and He should treat his peers in religion and in the world with respect. Another group of them believe that justice consists of: avoiding the great ones whom God has promised to punish them and not insisting on the small ones and avoiding any behavior against the merit and dignity of the group that he is inclined towards, but article 1705 of the Journal of Laws In the definition of Adel, he says: Adel is someone whose good deeds outweigh his bad deeds. Some Arabic-speaking jurists also believe that justice in Islamic jurisprudence is synonymous with good morals in civil law. Apart from the differences of opinion about the concept of justice in Islamic jurisprudence, different Islamic schools of thought also differ with each other regarding the requirement or non-requirement of justice, with the explanation that Malikiya, Shafi'i and Hanbaleh believe that justice is necessary for obtaining the position of judge, but The followers of the Hanafi religion believe that justice is not a condition for the administration of justice, nor is it even a condition for its influence and validity, rather they have considered it among the conditions of perfection. They have argued that a transgressor can also hold the position of judge. Because with them, the testimony of a transgressor is accepted, and because they say that whoever's testimony is accepted, his judgment will also be accepted. Therefore, they have accepted the administration of justice by Fasiq. It is interesting that after mentioning the above passages, they mentioned that it is appropriate not to judge the transgressor imam. Because judging is a huge and extensive provincial intervention and it does not deserve to be in the hands of those who do not have complete devotion and piety. Then they said that it is obligatory on the imam not to assign him to the work of judging, and rather this is forbidden and a sin for him, but if he assigns him to this task, the aforementioned appointment and his judgment are correct. However, most contemporary Arab writers have not accepted the opinion of Hanaf.

The second discourse: Imami jurisprudence

Imamiyyah jurists have considered the conditions necessary for a judge, so before entering into the discussion, it is appropriate to talk about the Shia's point of view about the position of a judge. In the customary definition of qadha in jurisprudence books such as Masalak and Tanqih, it is stated that the judgment consists of: Islamic guardianship over the verdict for someone who has the authority to issue a fatwa in the details of the Islamic laws, regarding certain people from the people based on proving their rights or fulfilling them for deserving in the book of lessons, it is stated that judgment consists of: sharia's authority over ruling and public interests on the part of the infallible imam.

In the analysis of the two definitions, sahib Jawahar says: we know that judgment is not synonymous with guardianship, and perhaps the mention of guardianship in the definitions is due to the fact that correct judgment is one of the ranks and positions of government and one of the branches of the genealogy of the public leadership of the holy prophet of Islam and his successors. In this case, the meaning of wilayat in the definition is either wilayat from God or wilayat from the prophet and imams.

In this way, it is clear that in the opinion of Shia jurists, judging is one of the branches of prophethood and imam, and just as the holy prophet and imams were taking steps in the direction of preserving the religion and divine values, the Islamic judge should also act in the direction of their guardianship and government be the guardian of the value system of Islam.

In support of this view, sahib Javaher explains the meaning of sufficient judgment and says: sufficient judgment is not a terminological meaning. One of the definite policies that the Imam must adopt is the appointment of persons through whom the system of mankind will be established. Moreover, it can be said that selecting the necessary number for this work is obligatory on the Imam and obligatory on those appointed by the imam. It can also be said that accepting the position of judge is obligatory from the imam.

From this statement, it is clear that judging is one of the functions of prophethood, imamate, and public leadership in religion and the world, and the fact that judges should be appointed by them is obvious, but rather frequent. During the time of imam Masoom's absence, jurists believe that the judgment of a jurist from the Ahl al-Bayt jurists is valid if it meets the conditions of the fatwa. In this case, such a jurist is authorized by the imams and appointed by them, which can be understood from the hadiths, therefore, the condition of installation or permission by the imam cannot be considered void.

Imamiyyah jurists have considered it mustahab to accept the judgment for someone who considers himself to be full of conditions, however, they have pointed out that the risk of doing this is huge and for someone who is not sure that he can fulfill its conditions, the first thing is to leave it. If he has knowledge of the lack of conditions, it becomes haram for him to judge.

Also, some jurists have considered the acceptance of qadha as a prelude to enjoining the good and forbidding the evil and rising in installments and therefore as a sufficient obligation, but the great Shia jurists have mentioned that whenever a person does not meet the conditions completely. For example, if he does not have sufficient knowledge and justice, and yet the imam chooses him to judge based on his interests, he can judge.

It has also been said that if an oppressor appoints a believer judge who has not reached the level of ijtihad and there is reluctance in this matter, the said person can accept the judgment, and some have said that it is obligatory to accept it in order to avoid harm, but it is necessary to that extent. Who is able to act and vote according to the right? In this way, we can see that the criterion of shia jurists in accepting and installing a judge is to uphold divine and religious rights and values, even some jurists have said that accepting a judgment from an oppressor for a mujtahid who is obligated to implement sharia rulings is not limited to reluctance, but rather It is obligatory to accept it. Because in this way, he finds an opportunity to put things in their place, enjoin good and forbid evil, and help the oppressed.

After mentioning the above introduction, it is necessary to check the conditions of the judge which are mentioned in the jurisprudence books. The jurists of Imamiyyah considered maturity, perfection of intellect, faith, justice, purity, knowledge, and being a man as prerequisites for a judge. Of course, it should be noted that the late holy Ardabili violated the third condition (faith) and the sixth condition (knowledge) and the author of Nahj al-Haq had legitimate doubts about his knowledge and manhood. Regarding the conditions of ijtihad, Sahib Javaher believes that judgment is not permissible for a person who is not knowledgeable and independent in issuing fatwas; ijtihad must be complete and ijtihad is not sufficient in some jurisprudence and jurisprudence chapters. In contrast to the above opinion, some people have said that what is used from the book and the sunnah is that the ruling from every believer is correct if it is based on truth, justice and installments.

In the end, sahib javaher believes that the claim of consensus on the condition of knowing ijtihad for the judge is not clear to me. Imamiyyah jurists have different opinions regarding the condition of recording, the power of writing and sight, but most of them do not consider them as conditions. It is also the power of the logic of speech and hearing that here some jurists have considered the application of the originality of the non-order of the effect in cases of doubt in the requirement.

The third speech: the conditions of the judge from Imam Ali's point of view

In his sermon to malik Ashtar Nakhai, the pious teacher hazrat Ali said about the conditions of a judge: "choose the one who is the best for you from among your subjects to judge between people. that things do not become difficult for him, and the struggle of his enemies does not lead him to stubbornness, and he does not persist in error, and when he knows the truth, he does not hesitate to return to it, and his soul does not turn to greed, and does not settle for a little knowledge until he reaches the truth, and does not dwell in doubts he was more cautious than anyone else and he used evidence more than anyone else, and he was less fed up with the comings and goings of the claimants, and he was more patient in revealing things, and when the ruling was clear, he was more decisive in judging.

Those who do not draw his praise well and welcome him, and these are few. So, judge such people and be generous in your forgiveness, so much so that his need for people will decrease and raise his rank in your eyes so that no one from your close ones will covet him and he will be safe from the sting of your men. In this regard, please note that this was caught in the hands of evildoers, who practiced idolatry in the name of religion and gained their world.

As we have seen, hazrat Ali paints a beautiful and enchanting picture of a pious scientist in front of his audience in his statement of the criteria for choosing a judge. Therefore, below, we will examine the characteristics of such a person according to the words of mullah motaqiyan. nowadays, in scientific circles, the characteristics of real scientists are less talked about, and this has caused confusion among people and officials. Therefore, we found it appropriate to express the characteristics of such people according to the experiences of the west and the east.

Experiences that seem to be taken from the words of hazrat Ali have been written in the role of portraying the character of the judge. Regarding the characteristics of a real scientist, some characteristics have been described as follows.

A) Possessing the power of thinking: Possessing the power of thinking depends on a strong and stimulated perception, a strong memory, and a high IQ, that is, the power of thinking is primarily due to the fact that all human objects, phenomena and events around a person are perceptual attractions for him. have and attract his attention and interest. In the next place, a person must have a strong memory to find the issues in a short time and finally to discover the connection between the issues with the power of his intelligence.

In the process of knowledge, a scientist usually deals with a confusing problem that others have difficulty in solving, although these problems are not always equally complicated. Therefore, in the discussion of the judicial organization, people should be classified according to their ability to solve all kinds of problems, but what we have said is not enough to make a thinker and problem solver, but the ability to think to other elements such as patience, perseverance, perseverance, struggle, austerity will be needed and these will be obtained when a person is a seeker and a lover.

B) Possessing intellectual structure: In addition to having the power of thinking and investigation, it is necessary for a scientist (judge) to have a suitable intellectual structure. One of our scientific problems, especially in law, compared to the West, is that some of our professors, despite their knowledge and information, do not have a coherent and interconnected, orderly and systematic intellectual structure. Some graduates have accumulated information and information that they can talk and write about for hours, but as soon as a problem is presented to them, they do not have the power to use the information and reasons learned in advance and cannot provide a specific solution.

Hazrat Ali says in this regard: A judge should be the one who uses evidence the most. Undoubtedly, applying evidence requires having an intellectual structure, and intellectual construction is the product of being taught by professors who pay attention to the most detailed points, individual components, and the logical connection between them and the whole complex at the same time, and know the logic of the legal system. This attribute is usually not achieved by personal effort and study and requires a student from the teacher. Therefore, in choosing a judge, we should pay attention to the university and the place of study and his professors.

C) Respect (justice): Other attributes mentioned by hazrat Ali can be summed up under the word's "respect" or "justice". Undoubtedly, in addition to scientific qualities, due to the difficulty of the work of judging and the fact that the act of interpretation is mixed with the framework of the judge's personality, it is necessary for him to have piety and asceticism. Otherwise, the beautiful face of Haq will not be revealed to him. Because God does not give his knowledge and wisdom to anyone, and one of the conditions for giving this gift is to have a refined and cultivated soul. Knowledge and piety are closely related, and true knowledge, which is light and enlightening, brings patience and high capacity, causes its owner to be stubborn with the truth and when he knows the truth, he returns to it, and worldly pursuits do not hinder his movement, but he must he noted that this knowledge can only be achieved by refining the soul and adorning it.

The third issue: methods of selecting prosecutor judges
Considering the position of the prosecutor in ensuring judicial independence, what can give objectivity and spirit to the necessary conditions for judges in practice is the way of prosecutor judges.
Ensuring the independence and impartiality of the judge in the pursuit of economic crimes in the administrative system, which is realized in terms of opinion through setting conditions for him, in terms of practice depends to a large extent on the methods of selecting and attracting judges, and if it is not done accurately and properly at this stage all theoretical discussions will remain sterile and fruitless. Therefore, in the continuation of the material, we will study the methods of selecting

the methods of selecting judges, including the prosecutor's judges in France and Iran. In general, in order for prosecutors to be able to pursue large economic crimes in the administrative system with the powers of the society that have great influence in the administrative system, they must be selected specifically. There are two general methods for selecting prosecutor judges: appointment and election.

A secondary question in this debate is whether prosecutorial judges should be selected from among members of the professional services (as in France and Germany), or from a specific group of lawyers (as in England), or, as in the United States, from any legal profession in general. Are they selected? The important content is that the importance of the position of the judiciary in the structure of the government provides the possibility of a moderate method of selection. According to the French tradition, the judicial system is part of the administrative hierarchy and therefore it is considered as a position or profession, but in common law, judges are chosen from those who work in judicial and legal professions, except for some state or district judges in the United States.

America In any case, in all three mentioned legal systems, judges are expected to be impartial people, and according to this, independence from the corrupt powers of the society, security and sanctity of their positions are guaranteed. In this way, it is clear that countries are often the same in their perception and view towards the judicial position, but they adopt different techniques and methods in the ways of attracting and employing suitable people for this position. Therefore, after mentioning the above introduction, it is appropriate to take a brief look at the practice of France and the Islamic republic of Iran regarding the methods of selecting judges.

The first speech: French procedure

Professional judges of the fifth republic are one of the criteria of the administrative apparatus. Therefore, they have a service period and retire after completing it. Like their British and American colleagues, they enjoy job security today. In France, an impartial judge is considered an ideal judge, and the judge's impartiality is highly valued. Although the minister of Justice is in charge of a part of the selection process of judges, political recommendations play a small role in their selection. All judges must have at least 28 months of training or judicial experience at the national judicial school in bordeaux.

Candidates for the position of judge in France enter the judicial system if they pass the competitive exam. Theoretically, according to the French constitution, the president of France is the guarantor and protector of the independence of the judiciary and chooses the judges, but in practice, the high-ranking judges are chosen by the supreme judicial council.

The supreme judicial council consists of the president, the minister of justice, and nine experienced lawyers who are elected by the president for a four-year term. This is done partly on the recommendation of the supreme court and the state council as follows: one person from the state council, three from the supreme court, three from other courts, and two people for their general qualifications. In any case, selective authorities have less power of selection than England and America.

The second speech: the practice of the Islamic Republic of Iran

In Iran, holders of a bachelor's degree in law or a bachelor's degree in theology or a bachelor's degree in the faculty of judicial and administrative sciences or holders of a judicial degree from the Qom higher judicial school can be elected to the position of assistant prosecutor if they have a diploma and pass the exam and if necessary, during the internship period.

Of course, the determination of the necessity of internship for judicial applicants and the duration of internship is left to the head of the judiciary. In 1998, according to the executive regulations of the law on the employment of judges and the conditions of internship, the selection and acceptance of qualified judicial interns was assigned to the general department of education, and the period of practical and scientific internship was set at a minimum of one year and a maximum of two years.

In April 2001, another regulation under the title of executive regulations of the law on selection and recruitment of judges was approved by the judiciary directorate, according to its article 2 and 3, the judiciary recruitment department annually announces the required number of judges to the department of selection and recruitment of judges in order to select and attract judicial staff.

After passing the scientific test, the candidates will be selected, if necessary, by the judge recruitment and selection department, and in this case, they will be introduced to the judiciary education general department to issue an internship notice. In this way, it can be seen that the method of selecting judges in Iran is somewhat similar to the method of France, with the difference that in the selection of judges in Iran, like in France, the opinions of experts and experienced people are not considered to attract competent people. It is appropriate that changes should be made in the entrance exams at least to get closer to the international standards and the desirable and worthy judging system of the Islamic system.

Among other things, in the entrance exams, the candidates' ability to reason and infer and understand the law and the conditions that we have mentioned in the previous discussions should be properly tested, which can undoubtedly be done by holding four-choice exams and questions that are exactly the repetition of legal articles. will not be. It is also appropriate to carefully consider the criteria from the words of hazrat Ali in the selection of judges, including prosecution judges, so that we can witness the employment of competent and competent judges.

Finally, it is worth noting that attracting competent and competent people requires that, with the measures taken by the authorities, the position of judge, both in terms of social attitude and in terms of meeting the material and spiritual needs of honorable judges, finds its proper and real position so that people with intelligence and have a strong motivation to enter this sensitive position with tact and competence. In the field of social life, the law, as the crystallization of the normative system, is not always representative of the value system, but under the influence of the influence and inductions of social forces, it may represent the result of the interests and attitudes of the forces from the society, which are necessarily related to the value system reflected in the constitution or public beliefs and Elahi are not aligned and aligned, to compensate for this shortcoming in the legislative process based on some interpretation methods, we recommend that legal regulations be interpreted based on the logic of needs and especially in line with social values and the requirements of justice and fairness.

Based on this approach, the role of the judge in maintaining the value system is well known. For this reason, most countries place special emphasis on considering the scientific and moral qualifications of judges. Apart from this, some thinkers consider the influence of unconscious factors to be very decisive in judicial reasoning.

Therefore, they insist on a special judgment to evaluate the candidates' personality. The scientific and moral qualifications of judges are to a large extent in the quality of the educational environment and teaching and study materials and the way professors of law schools teach.

Naturally, one of the most effective guarantees in training competent judges is the existence of a dynamic and appropriate educational system, which we discussed some of its features. Through comparative studies, it has been found that all countries, in addition to having scientific qualifications, also consider good manners and good manners as a condition for selecting a judge, and they place special emphasis on this matter in the selection of judges.

Especially in the Islamic jurisprudence system, which considers the prosecutor not a job, but a kind of reward or mission. Regarding scientific qualifications, the countries under the common law system, in addition to legal knowledge, consider it a condition to have insight and experience in various fields of social life, and considering the statements of Hazrat Ali in Nahj al-Balagha, it seems that the prosecutor of the Islamic government should also have such characteristics.

The second topic: the role of employees and prosecutor's assistants in the pursuit of economic crimes

Among the employees and judicial assistants, a group works in the process of determining the issue, and another group directs the case both in the phase of determining the issue and the verdict, and another group works in the classification of verdicts and archiving and preparing the case for the issuance of the verdict. Therefore, you can see that one of the critical issues in the pursuit of economic crimes is the issue of employees and assistants of the prosecutor's office. Although the mentioned people are not decision-makers, their actions and actions play a very effective and strong role in directing the decision-making process of the prosecutor's judge.

Because, as we know, the sentence and the issue are inseparable, and if the aforementioned people do not correctly and completely reflect the example of the issue, which is a real and objective matter, no doubt the prosecutor's judge, no matter how competent and knowledgeable he is about the legal rulings, will go wrong and issue an unjust verdict, while apparently the inference is correct. Maintaining the society's value system based on the standards of justice is closely related to the performance of judicial employees and assistants. In general, the persons who help the judge in filing and completing the case and preparing it for issuing a verdict are classified into two groups in terms of their employment relationship with the judicial system:

- ❖ Employees who are employed and paid by the government or judicial system.
- ❖ Judicial assistants who are not paid by the government or judicial system.

The first speech: Employees

Receiving petitions and bills and attached documents, recording them in special offices, setting the time for processing and serving them, and arranging the documents of the cases in an accurate and easy-to-access manner requires the existence of administrative organizations and the employment of people other than prosecutors. Since the initiation of proceedings, as well as the collection and coordination of documents and reasons, and generally providing the basis for issuing a correct and fair verdict, depends on the performance of court employees. The selection of competent, accurate, orderly, impartial and persistent people has a direct effect on the smooth flow of affairs in the prosecutor's office in the pursuit of economic crimes.

Referees to the judiciary face the judicial staff before filing a lawsuit before the judge, and the type of performance and treatment of the aforementioned persons plays a very important role in speeding up the proceedings and the feeling of safety and satisfaction of the referrals. In articles 81, 82 and 84 of the Law on the principles of judicial organizations approved in 1929, it is stated that in each court or its branch, there is an office manager to organize the cases and prepare the proceedings according to the procedure prescribed in the Law on the Principles of Trials and under the leadership and responsibility of the head of the court. (Head of the branch) performs his duties. According to article 82, the director of the office will have enough scribes, stability and bailiffs under his leadership and responsibility as determined by the minister of Justice.

Of course, it is worth mentioning that according to the opinion of some professors, the head of the branch is responsible for monitoring the performance of the office manager, etc. French authors also believe that the administration of court affairs requires the existence of an administrative structure so that the following tasks can be performed well:

- ❖ Categorizing and archiving the rulings of dadiari branches.
- ❖ Preparing and maintaining files, registers and lists and performing some actions such as summoning the parties, serving the documents of the

petition and sometimes serving the judgment, which of course, the latter
issues are possible in low-cost and easy-to-find lawsuits.

- ❖ Carrying out some extrajudicial duties such as dealing with personal registration offices and taking care of them, receiving declarations, maintaining commercial offices, registering commercial securities and the like.
- ❖ French authors believe that in a large court the favorable administration of justice is related to the proper functioning of the court office.

The second speech: assistants of justice

In addition to judicial officers, other persons also assist the prosecutor in the pursuit of economic crimes in the performance of judicial duties, among which lawyers and official judicial experts can be mentioned.

A) Lawyers: By providing their legal advice and guidance, lawyers clarify the course and framework of the value system for their clients when they suffer from economic crimes and explain to them the ways of enjoying the support of the judicial system. Also, in the position of filing a lawsuit, they prepare the case for prosecution by presenting documents and citing legal materials. Their presence in the proceedings prevents the possible arbitrariness of the judges, and in this sense, lawyers are not only colleagues of the judicial system, but they are considered an obstacle in the way of the prosecutor's arbitrariness, and they play an important role in the formation of a just and fair trial. It is precisely because of this mutual possibility that thinkers have proposed the independence of the attorney and some provisions so that the citizens have a shelter and refuge against the possible tyranny of the judicial system and especially the fictional institution.

B) Official experts: in a large number of judicial cases, due to the specialized or technical nature of the issues and relationships between persons, the prosecutor alone is not able to fully and accurately understand the issues or relationships. For this reason, in many cases, the prosecutor officially asks for the opinion of the experts by issuing an expert opinion, so that according to their reports, he can correctly identify the issue and issue a competent and fair decision. For this reason, experts have been considered as judicial assistants. Expertise, as they say in French law, is a temporary duty and function and not a job. Because the expert is chosen at some point in time by the judge or litigants.

Chapter IV

Conclusion

With the recognition of the rule of declaring a public crime and the separation of the divine aspect of crimes from their private aspect in Islamic law, this distinction and separation has also been reflected in the laws of our country, and public lawsuits have found separate coordinates from private lawsuits. Since the mixed system was accepted in the judicial process of our country and the institution of prosecution was separated from the institution of hearing and issuing judgments. The prosecutor's office was placed under the supervision of the court and the matter of pursuing the general aspect of the crime was entrusted to the prosecutor's office. As it was said, one of the basic and important factors in preventing and fighting economic corruption among official and unofficial institutions is the development and strengthening of legalism. One of the essentials for the development and strengthening of legalism in the country is the existence of supervisory authorities and institutions. Because these institutions, like precise and regular observers, regularly review and evaluate the routine and flow of affairs so that they do not deviate from the legal path. Therefore, in line with this, the fictional organization should have both natural supervision and, if it observes a specific case, prosecute it under the rights of the society. On the other hand, due to the fact that economic crimes are sometimes caused by people who are connected to administrative centers and sources of power, therefore, the implementation of an effective monitoring system by story is subject to special conditions that require expert, caring, ethical and experienced forces. Corruption is one of the serious harms that can happen even to an observer who is sent to investigate and control corruption. Accepting bribes, party playing and conflict of interests are among the things that double the importance of selection and selection of people in the matter of supervision. First of all, the prosecutor must have full knowledge and respect for the issue of surveillance so that he can evaluate the issue of surveillance from different dimensions and possibly different appearances and incorrect information will not distract him from the reality of the matter. He should be well aware of the relevant laws and be able to give an opinion on how to properly implement them. On the other hand, he must have a high understanding and superior moral character in order to have the task of pursuing and fighting this particular type of crimes, he must have high interest and motivation in his performance and believe in his work so that don't be hesitant, negligent and indulgent, or succumb to temptations and threats. Unfortunately, the lack of experienced manpower in the prosecution institution as a result of the use of untrained and inexperienced forces has made the issue face extremes in practice, which has ultimately caused dissatisfaction, discouragement and pessimism among the managers of various institutions and institutions in different departments.

Proposals

Today, all institutions are trying to find a representative or an office for themselves in the judicial authorities, while it is the prosecutor who should have representatives in the important financial authorities and centers to enable monitoring, follow-up and even fight. This legal objection may be raised that despite the existence of monitoring centers such as the national inspection Organization, it is unnecessary to provide a position for the prosecutor's representatives. As an answer to such objection, the duties of the judiciary can be referred to in article 156 of the constitution. Also, according to article 3 of the law amending the law on establishing public courts and the revolution approved in 2003, one of the tasks of the prosecutor is to detect crimes, including economic crimes, predicting such a task for the judiciary requires the preparation of reasons to enter this area.

Resources

Ansari, Baqir, The role of the judge in the transformation of the judicial system, Tehran, Mizan, 2017.

Olsen, Vankor, power and prosperity, communist growth and tyranny of capitalism, translated by Manouchehr Farhang, Tehran, Higher Institute of Management and Planning Education and Research, 2007.

Al Hart, Richart, organization, structure, process and methods, translated by Ali Parsaian and Seyyed Mohammad Arabi and cultural research office, Tehran, 4th edition, 2014.

Tank, Andre, Laws of the United States of America, translated by Seyyed Hossein Safaei, Tehran, Institute of Comparative Law, 1980.

Jafari Tabar, Hassan, Philosophical Foundations of Legal Interpretation, Tehran, Publishing Company, 2013.

Javadi Amoli, Abdullah, series of debates on the philosophy of religion, philosophy of human rights, Isra, 1997.

J. M. Sheffertiz and J. Steven: Theory of Organizations: Myths, translated by Ali Parsaviyan, Tomeh, 2011.

Hakimi, Mohammad, Defending Women's Rights, Farhang Islamic Publishing House, second edition, 2012.

Hamidian, Hassan, Control of the Legislature in Iran and America. Nair, 2000.

Delavi, Mohammad Reza and Mehdi Jamshidian, Fundamentals of Organization and Management, Tehran, Simin, 2002.

Dutoqueville, Alexey, Analysis of Democracy in America, translated by Rahmat Elah Moghadam Maraghaei, Tehran, Scientific and Cultural Publishing Company, 2004.

Domichel, Andre and Lamelomir, Pierre, Public Law, Abolfazl Ghazi Shariat Panahi, Tehran, Gostar, 1998.

Russell, Bertrand, Power, translated by Najaf Daryabandari, Tehran, Kharazmi, 1990.

Rain, Alan, Philosophy of Social Sciences, translated by Abdul Karim Soroush, Sarat Cultural Institute, Tehran, third edition, 1994.

Reinhard Bendix, The Thought of Max Weber, translated by Mahmoud Rambad, Tehran, Hermes, 1994.

Rafipour, Faramarz, Anatomy of society, Tehran, publishing company.

Roger, Peru, French judicial institutions, translated by Shahram Ebrahimi, Abbas Tadin and Gholam Hossein Koshki, Tehran, Selsbil Publishing, 2014.

Zarang, Mohammad, History of the Constitution in the three countries of Iran, France and America, Tehran, Islamic Revolution Documentation Center, 2006.

Shams, Abdullah, Code of Civil Procedure, Volume 1, Tehran, Mizan Publishing House, 2002.

Sheikhul-Islami, Seyyed Mohsen, Comparative Constitutional Law, Constitutional Law of England, United States of America, France, Germany, Kushamher Publications, 2002.

Sanei, Parviz, Law and Society, the relationship between law and social and psychological factors, Tehran, New Design, 2013.

Sahife Noor, Tehran, Ministry of Islamic Guidance Printing Company, 1984.

Erfani, Mahmoud, Comparative Law, Contemporary Legal Systems, Tehran, Jungle Publications, 2015.

Alam, Mahmoud, Standard Justice in International Documents, Tehran, Mizan Publishing, 2014.

Ali Dost, Abu al-Qasim, Fiqh and Custom, Research Institute of Islamic Culture and Thought, first edition 2014.

Farkman, Anke and Gerish Thomas, Justice in Germany, translated by Mohammad Reza Dari, Tahhidkhaneh and Hamidreza Behermand Bag Nazar, Tehran, Samt Publications, 2012.

Judge Shariat Panahi, Abolfazl, Constitutional Rights and Political Institutions, Volume 1, Tehran University Publications, March 2016.

Judge Shariat Panahi, Abolfazl, Basic Rights Basics, Tehran, Mizan Publishing House, 8th edition, 2003.

Qolipour, Arin, Institutions and Organizations, Institutional Ecology of Organizations, Tehran, Samet Publications, 2014.

Constitution of France and Italy, published by the General Administration of Laws and Regulations of the country, 1998.

Kelly. John, A Brief History of Legal Theory in the West, translated by Mohammad Rasakh, New Plan Publishing, Tehran, 2012.

Katouzian, Nasser, Philosophy of Law, volume 1, Tehran, publishing company, first edition, 1999.

Katouzian, Nasser, Generalities of Law, General Theory, Tehran, Publishing Company, first edition, 2001.

Caton, Aliot and Katherman Vernon, French legal system, translated by Safar Beyzadeh, Tehran, Majlis Research Center, 2012.

Galbraith, John Kenneth, Anatomy of Power, translated by Dr. Ahmed Shahsa, published by Nagaresh, 1992.

Nabavi, Seyyed Abbas, Philosophy of Power, Tehran, Samit Publications, 2001.

Vakil, Amir Saed and Asgari, Pouria, the Constitution in the current legal system, Tehran, Majd Scientific and Cultural Forum, 2011.

Wayne St. Andrew, State theories, translated by Hossein Bashiriyeh, Ney Publishing, 1994.

Hashemi, Seyyed Mohammad, Fundamental Rights of the Islamic Republic of Iran, Volume 2, Governance and Political Institutions and Shahid Beheshti University Publications, Tehran in collaboration with Yalda Publishing, 1994.

Yazdi, Mohammad, The Constitution for All, Tehran, Amir Kabir Publishing House, 1995.

yes I want morebooks!

Buy your books fast and straightforward online - at one of world's fastest growing online book stores! Environmentally sound due to Print-on-Demand technologies.

Buy your books online at
www.morebooks.shop

Kaufen Sie Ihre Bücher schnell und unkompliziert online – auf einer der am schnellsten wachsenden Buchhandelsplattformen weltweit! Dank Print-On-Demand umwelt- und ressourcenschonend produzi ert.

Bücher schneller online kaufen
www.morebooks.shop

Printed by Books on Demand GmbH, Norderstedt / Germany